COOKING FOR *Life*

RECIPES

FOR

HEALTHY

LIVING

VOLUME 3

COOKING FOR *Life*

Recipes for Healthy Living

Published by Avera McKennan Foundation

Copyright © 2007 by
Avera McKennan Foundation
800 East 21st Street
Sioux Falls, South Dakota 57105

This cookbook is a collection of favorite recipes,
which are not necessarily original recipes.

Library of Congress Catalog Number: 2005932869
ISBN: 0-9760598-2-7

Edited and Manufactured by
Favorite Recipes® Press
An imprint of

FRP™

P.O. Box 305142
Nashville, Tennessee 37230
800-358-0560

Art Director: Steve Newman
Project Editor: Debbie Van Mol, RD

First Printing: 2007   7,500 copies

Printed in China

Contributors

Project Managers: Tina Ames
                             Ann Carroll

Recipe Development
  and Editing: Tami Gangestad, MS, RD, CNSD, LN
                             Mary Lobb Oyos, RN, BC-ADM, CDE
                             Ginger Trumbull, RD, LN, CDE
                             Nancy Bertsch, RD, LN
                             Food Service Team of the Avera Heart Hospital
                               of South Dakota

Contributing Editors: Mary Michaels
                             Nancy Bertsch, RD, LN
                             Ann Wipf, RD, LN, CDE

Project Advisor: Jennifer Cisar

Book Design: Henkin Schultz Communication Arts

Illustrations and
  Photography: © Henkin Schultz Communication Arts

Left to right: Mary Lobb Oyos, RN, BC ADM, CDE;
Paul Luttman, Chef; Nancy Bertsch, RD, LN

But those who hope in the LORD will renew their strength. They will soar on wings like eagles; they will run and not grow weary, they will walk and not be faint.

Isaiah 40:31

Contents

Foreword

Diabetes is a very common disease, affecting over eighteen million Americans, or more than 6 percent of the population. One-third of the people who have diabetes are not even aware of it.

During the more than twenty years I've worked as a diabetes nurse, so much has changed, but much has stayed the same. Technology has advanced dramatically, making it much easier for people with diabetes to check their blood sugar and take insulin. The number of medications available for glucose control has also increased. Diabetes is still a very challenging disease, however. Healthy eating and regular activity remain the cornerstones of diabetes management.

Successful diabetes care involves teamwork, flexibility, determination, and lifestyle changes. Over the years, I have been very privileged to work with countless people who meet these challenges every day and strive to achieve the best blood sugar control possible. From a two-year-old and his parents who learn the complexities of an insulin pump to the ninety-year-old who is newly diagnosed and learns to check his or her blood sugar, the faces of diabetics cover every segment of the population.

Our diabetes team has been inspired by children who give their own insulin injections for the first time. We have celebrated with women who have had diabetes during pregnancy and worked so hard to deliver a healthy baby. We have provided many people with the information and skills to live successfully with diabetes.

COOKING FOR LIFE is designed for all of these people and their families. Our team of diabetes experts is dedicated to caring for people with diabetes in the region, and this cookbook is one more way we can express that caring. Some of these recipes have been enjoyed by our Diabetes Support Group members and participants at our quarterly Living with Diabetes programs.

All proceeds from this cookbook are donated to the Avera McKennan Diabetes Care Fund, where they will be used for education and other services for people with diabetes.

Living with diabetes is a journey, not a destination. Wishing you strength, good health, and support in your journey. Happy cooking!

Mary Lobb Oyos

Mary Lobb Oyos, RN, BC-ADM, CDE
Diabetes Program Manager

Dedication

This cookbook is dedicated to the men, women, and children with diabetes and their families. We recognize and honor you as you strive for a healthy diet while managing diabetes in your daily lives.

This cookbook is also dedicated to the team of health professionals at Avera Endocrinology, Avera Children's, and Avera Diabetes Education Services who work every day to help raise awareness of diabetes prevention and who care for individuals with diabetes throughout our region.

Preface

Diabetes—Hearing the diagnosis for the first time brings a range of feelings, emotions, and questions. How will this affect my life? Will I need insulin? Can my child still participate in sports? What can I eat?

The days and months after a diabetes diagnosis are filled with new routines and lots of information. As we talk about the adjustment to diabetes in our Diabetes Self-Management classes, most people identify food-related issues as the hardest thing about living with diabetes.

Food is an important part of our culture—in social gatherings, as a source of comfort, and as a necessity for survival. Our eating habits and customs are part of who we are, and when diabetes requires a change in what's familiar to us, that is understandably difficult.

However, diabetes can actually provide a wonderful opportunity for a healthier lifestyle. Planning meals with diabetes today is all about what you CAN eat, not what is "forbidden." It's about being well informed and making healthy choices.

Our team of diabetes nurses, dietitians, and chefs worked together to provide a wonderful selection of recipes that will appeal to every member of the family. Each recipe has detailed nutrition information that includes both carbohydrate choices and grams to make meal planning and carbohydrate counting easier.

COOKING FOR LIFE is for the whole family, whether they have diabetes or not. Although some special considerations should be made, a person with diabetes can enjoy all of the social, traditional, and flavorful aspects that surround food. Families can enjoy the pleasure of cooking and eating meals together often. Research shows many advantages to families eating together five or more times per week, including:

- family bonding through conversation

- better nutrition

- better academic performance and emotional well-being in children and teens

- lower incidence of substance abuse in teens

- continuation of family traditions and favorite recipes

We hope the recipes in COOKING FOR LIFE will help bring families together to enjoy some delicious and creative dishes.

• Diabetes Support Group—Meets monthly except in the summer.

• Quarterly Living with Diabetes programs.

You can also find diabetes information on our Web site at www.averamckennan.org.

Eating Healthy
With Diabetes

Diabetes is a disease in which the body does not make or use insulin properly. This results in high blood glucose (sugar) levels. When we eat, part of the food is broken down into glucose. Some of this glucose is used immediately for energy, while the remainder is stored in muscle and fat tissue for later use. Insulin, a hormone produced by the pancreas, is released in response to blood glucose changes. Insulin goes to the body cells and works like a key to unlock the cell doors and allow the glucose to enter. When a person has diabetes, something in this process does not work effectively.

Millions of Americans also have pre-diabetes. With this condition, blood glucose levels are not normal, yet they are not high enough to make the diagnosis of diabetes. Two major studies revealed that for people with pre-diabetes, positive lifestyle changes can reduce the risk of developing type 2 diabetes by 58 percent.

Healthy eating and regular physical activity are the cornerstones of diabetes self-care. Achieving the right balance of foods in the appropriate amounts and at regular times throughout the day can keep glucose levels more consistent.

A healthy diet for diabetics embraces the same healthy eating guidelines recommended for everyone. Contrary to common beliefs, a person with diabetes does not have to eat special foods or eliminate certain foods entirely. In fact, there are no foods that the person with diabetes can't eat. Moderation is the key. This section highlights the benefits of eating a healthy balanced diet that includes a variety of foods to promote good nutrition and optimal health. It also includes carbohydrate counting information and a guide to using the symbols on the recipe pages to assist in carbohydrate source recognition and counting carbohydrate "choices" to better control diabetes.

What Is a Healthy Diet?

A healthy eating pattern is one that includes regular meals and snacks and contains a variety of foods for balanced nutrition. The following recommendations are good habits whether you have diabetes or not:

Don't skip meals.
- Regular meals promote optimal metabolism and provide the fuel needed for daily activity—both physical and mental. Skipping meals often leads to overeating later, which can lead to unwanted weight gain.
- If you have diabetes, skipping meals makes it difficult to maintain stable blood sugars. Work with your healthcare team to establish consistent mealtimes that work with your lifestyle.

Monitor portion sizes.
- Meals with moderate portions of a variety of foods prevent excessive calorie intake while providing the most nutrition. This promotes better nutrition and weight management.

Eat a variety of foods.
- Different foods contain different kinds of valuable nutrients. Eating a diet rich in grains, fruits, vegetables, dairy, and protein sources ensures that the body gets the nutrients it needs each day.
- Getting a balance of proteins, carbohydrates, and fats at meals through a variety of food groups promotes satiety (the fullness factor) and a more gradual breakdown of food into energy or glucose—especially beneficial for people with diabetes.

Limit "empty" calories.
- Overconsumption of foods with added sugars can contribute to calorie overload while providing little, if any, of the essential nutrients.
- If you have diabetes, consuming sugary foods and beverages can make it difficult to stay within your carbohydrate goals. For example, a 16-ounce bottle of regular cola provides 200 calories, no vitamins or minerals, and 52 grams of carbohydrate from sugar. That's the same carbohydrate as a meal that includes a whole sandwich, a salad, a piece of fruit, and unsweetened iced tea!

Nutrition

The Big Three: Proteins, Fats, and Carbohydrates

We get our energy, or calories, from three main nutrients called macronutrients—proteins, fats, and carbohydrates. They all work together to promote satiety and provide all the key nutrients the body needs.

Protein supports the body's repair and maintenance. Protein foods should make up about 10 to 30 percent of our daily calories, and they provide 4 calories per gram.

Making good protein choices:

- Monitor your portion size. A 3-ounce serving is about the size of a deck of cards.
- Choose the leanest cuts of beef and pork, like round and loin.
- Trim visible fat from meat before cooking.
- Choose extra-lean ground beef (90 percent lean or better).
- Remove the skin from poultry before eating.
- Choose lean deli meats like turkey, roast beef, ham, or pork loin instead of bologna or salami.
- Broil, grill, roast, poach, or boil meat, poultry, or fish instead of frying.
- Limit breaded and fried meat, poultry, or fish.

The American diet tends to contain more red meats like beef and pork, some poultry, and occasionally fish. The 2005 Dietary Guidelines encourage us to vary our protein choices to include more fish, nuts, and beans (like kidney, pinto, black, white, lentils, garbanzo, and soy) for their health benefits and to help us to cut down on saturated fat in our diet.

Fats and oils should make up 20 to 35 percent of calories in a healthy diet. Since they provide twice the amount of calories per gram as proteins or carbohydrates, they provide satiety (fullness). They also help our bodies carry and absorb fat-soluble vitamins like A, D, E, and K, and they play a role in numerous body functions.

Solid fats include animal fats and trans fats. Animal fats contain mostly saturated fat, and they also contain cholesterol. Trans fats have been found to affect cholesterol levels more negatively than saturated fat. Because of the concern over trans fats and our health, the FDA (Food and Drug Administration) has mandated that trans fats be listed in grams on the Nutrition Facts label by 2006.

Oils (unsaturated fats that are liquid at room temperature) come from many different sources like rapeseed (canola), soybeans (vegetable), corn, olives, nuts and seeds, avocados, ground flax, and fish. A few plant oils such as coconut oil and palm kernel oil are very high in saturated fats and should be used very sparingly.

Making good fat choices:
- Limit saturated fats by using only small amounts of butter and enjoying moderate portions of lean meats and poultry, trimming fat and removing poultry skin.
- Use lean cooking methods like grilling and broiling.
- Skim the fat that floats to the top when using a moist cooking method, such as when preparing a roast.
- To decrease the intake of trans fats, choose oils and trans-fat-free margarines instead of stick margarine.
- Since hydrogenated (trans) fats and tropical oils are often used to give flavor, stability, and longer shelf life to packaged products and snacks, replace these snacks with fruits, vegetables, whole grains, and nuts.
- Choose more whole foods and do more home cooking.
- Use beneficial plant oils like canola and olive and enjoy moderate portions of nuts and avocados for their beneficial fats.
- Include plant sources of Omega-3s (they contain alpha linolenic acid, which converts to healthful Omega-3s in the body) like canola oil, walnuts, and ground flaxseed as well as foods like Omega-3-enhanced eggs.
- Consider therapeutic margarine spreads that contain plant stanols or sterols, a plant component that can lower LDL cholesterol 10 to 14 percent.

Nutrition

Carbohydrates in a healthy diet should make up about half our calories (45 to 60 percent). They are our primary energy source and provide important vitamins, minerals, and fiber. Carbohydrate foods include grains and grain-based foods, fruits, some vegetables, milk, and yogurt. Sweets are also sources of carbohydrate, but provide little nutrition value other than calories.

Grains
Grain foods (breads, cereals, pasta, rice, and other grains) provide energy, vitamins, and minerals. Based on a 2,000-calorie diet, we should consume six servings per day.* Whole grains (grains that haven't had the bran processed out of them) provide additional benefits including fiber, original vitamins, and minerals and phytochemicals (plant compounds) that reduce the risk of several chronic diseases.

Fruits and vegetables
Studies show those who eat generous amounts of fruits and vegetables as part of a healthful diet are likely to have reduced risk of chronic diseases, including stroke and other cardiovascular diseases, type 2 diabetes, and certain cancers. In the 2005 Dietary Guidelines for Americans reference 2000-calorie diet, we are encouraged to take in two cups of fruit and two and one-half cups of vegetables per day.*

Milk and milk products
Milk and milk products, including yogurt and cheese, provide high-quality protein, vitamins, and minerals. A diet rich in milk and milk products can reduce the risk of low bone mass throughout the life cycle, which is especially important for children and adolescents who are building their peak bone mass and developing lifelong habits. Optimal intake for individuals over the age of eight is three servings of dairy per day.

* *Serving recommendations may be lower or higher depending on calorie needs.*

Carbohydrate and Diabetes

Carbohydrate is the main source of glucose in the body, since it is primarily the carbohydrate in the diet that breaks down into blood glucose or sugar. If you have diabetes, you need to pay attention to how much carbohydrate you consume in a meal and balance that with your medication and activity.

Is a low carbohydrate diet what you're after? No.

At a similar calorie level, your carbohydrate needs are similar to those for someone who does not have diabetes. It is the *distribution* of these foods throughout the day and staying consistent with your carbohydrate portions that are most important to help control blood glucose levels if you have diabetes. A typical meal plan includes three to five servings, or "choices," of carbohydrates for meals and one to two servings for snacks (if snacks are included in your plan). Work with your dietitian to develop a plan based on your calorie and nutrient needs, food preferences, and lifestyle.

Carbohydrate Counting

An excellent way to monitor carbohydrate intake is "carbohydrate counting." This lets you eat the foods you enjoy, even desserts, because you will know how they fit into your plan!

Two methods of carbohydrate counting:

- Carbohydrate "choices" (also known as exchanges)

- Carbohydrate grams

Nutrition

Counting Carbohydrate Choices

A carbohydrate choice equals 15 grams of carbohydrate. With the "choice" method of carb counting, you do not count protein or fat sources, non-starchy vegetables, or "free" foods. Also, total carbohydrate in an item is rounded to the nearest 15-gram amount. For example:

Food	Carbohydrate Choices
1/2 banana	1
2 slices wheat toast	2
2 Tbsp. peanut butter	0
8 oz. 1% milk	1
1 cup coffee	0
Total choices for breakfast	4

1 choice = 15 grams. Therefore, at this meal, you have 4x15=60 grams of carbohydrates.

Using a constant number of carbohydrate choices for meals and snacks is like having a carbohydrate "budget," and you choose how to spend it. Learn the choice numbers and serving sizes for foods you eat often so that it becomes second nature. You'll be able to estimate what's on your plate and make adjustments as you go.

Counting Carbohydrate Grams

Many people with diabetes prefer to count grams of carbohydrate for greater accuracy regarding insulin dosing or for other reasons. There are many useful tools to assist a person with this, such as pocket-size food composition books, Web sites, computer and PDA software, and, of course, food labels. When counting grams, carbohydrate amounts are not rounded up or down as in the choice or exchange method. Counting grams of carbohydrate might look like this:

Food	Carbohydrate Grams
1/2 banana	15
2 slices wheat toast	27
2 Tbsp. peanut butter	5
8 oz. 1% milk	12

Total grams for breakfast = 59

Sources of Carbohydrate

Look for the bolded symbols of these foods on the recipe pages to indicate the sources of carbohydrate in the recipes, as well as the total amount of carbohydrate in grams and in "choices."

Grains: breads, cereals, pasta, rice, other grain foods

Starchy vegetables: corn, potato, peas, winter squash, and dried beans

Milk and yogurt

Fruits and fruit juices

Sweets

Another thing you will find on the recipe pages is the nutritional analysis for the recipe (see sample below). Not all recipes are intended to be low in sodium or fat. The nutritional analysis is provided to help you know how you can fit the foods into your healthy diet. For example, items higher in fat or sodium should be paired with lower fat/lower sodium foods. For example, one portion of Satay Beef Kabobs on page 30 has 64 percent of its calories from fat, but served with a cup of vegetables, 8 ounces of skim milk, and a slice of whole grain bread = 30 percent calories from fat.

NUTRIENTS PER SERVING   Yield: 4 servings

CAL	PROT	CARBO	T FAT	SAT. FAT	MONOUFA	FIBER	SOD	OMEGA-3 FA	K
188	7G	27G	5G	3G	‹1G	0G	97MG	0G	223MG

PER SERVING	CARB CHOICES	3	CARB SOURCES				

Nutrition Facts

Serving Size 7 Crackers (29g)
Servings Per Container About 8

Amount Per Serving

Calories 120   Calories from Fat 25

	% **Daily Value***
Total Fat 3g	**5**%
Saturated Fat 0g	**0**%
Trans Fat 0g	
Polyunsaturated Fat 1.5g	
Monounsaturated Fat 0.5g	
Cholesterol 0mg	**0**%
Sodium 160mg	**6**%
Total Carbohydrate 21g	**7**%
Dietary Fiber 3g	**13**%
Sugars 0g	
Protein 3g	

Vitamin A 0%	•	Vitamin C 0%
Calcium 0%	•	Iron 6%

*Percent Daily Values are based on a 2,000 calorie diet. Your daily values may be higher or lower depending on your calorie needs:

	Calories	2,000	2,500
Total Fat	Less than	65g	80g
Sat Fat	Less than	20g	25g
Cholesterol	Less than	300mg	300mg
Sodium	Less than	2,400mg	2,400mg
Total Carbohydrate		300g	375g
Dietary Fiber		25g	30g

Label Reading

The Nutrition Facts label on packaged products can give you the information you need to count carbohydrate choices.

First, note the serving size, since all of the nutrition information on the label is related to that portion.

Second, look at the grams of total carbohydrate. Resist the temptation to count only the sugar grams. Total carbohydrate includes the starch (grain, starchy vegetable), fruit, and dairy carbohydrate in the food or beverage as well as the added sugars.

If you are counting carbohydrate choices, you can next determine how many choices you are getting by dividing the total carbohydrate grams by 15. Remember: If you intend to consume twice the listed portion size, you'll need to double the grams of carbohydrate before dividing by 15. Once you find out the number of choices you're eating, you know how it fits into your plan.

More About Fiber

Dietary fiber (soluble and insoluble) in the diet is associated with decreased risk for heart disease, optimal bowel function, weight management, blood glucose control, and cancer prevention. Foods high in dietary fiber, like whole grains, whole fruits and vegetables, and dried beans and peas, are digested more slowly, providing a lasting feeling of fullness without excess calories. In addition, high fiber foods have a more gradual breakdown into blood glucose, which promotes less rapid rises in blood glucose after a meal. If a food contains a significant amount (5 or more grams) of dietary fiber per serving, you may subtract these grams from the total carbohydrate before calculating the number of carbohydrate "choices" or grams you're getting. For example, if a food has 24 grams total carbohydrate and 9 grams dietary fiber, subtract 9 from 24 and you have 15 grams carbohydrate, or 1 carb choice.

What About Sweets?

One of the advantages of counting carbs is that you will know how sweets fit into your plan. To allow for dessert at a meal, you may choose to "trade" other carbohydrate choices for the treats to stay within your goals. Or you may take extra insulin to cover the additional carbohydrate. If you do happen to go over your carbohydrate goal at your meal, you may be able to add some physical activity after the meal to help lower your blood sugar. Just take care not to go overboard in the number of or portion size of sweets. Keep in mind that sweets and desserts add sugar and fat calories and, therefore, can cause unwanted weight gain. They may also compromise nutrition if they replace more healthful sources of carbohydrate too often. Many times a piece of fruit or a sugar-free yogurt can satisfy a sweet tooth and provide nutrition at the same time.

Sugar Substitutes

There are many "non-nutritive" sweeteners, or sugar substitutes, available. Sugar substitutes are high-intensity sweeteners that have few or no calories or glycemic response. Examples of sugar substitutes include:

Acesulfame K—Sunett or Sweet One

Aspartame—NutraSweet or Equal

Saccharin—Sweet 'n Low or Sugar Twin

Sucralose—Splenda

Sugar substitutes may help eliminate the need to add table sugar or honey to beverages or cereal. However, many foods that contain sugar substitutes still have calories and carbohydrate, so they can affect blood sugar. Sometimes there is very little difference in the calories or total carbohydrate in sugar-free foods compared to a small portion of "regular" foods.

Nutrition

Children with Diabetes

Living with diabetes is challenging for everyone, but especially for children with diabetes and their parents. School parties, trick-or-treating, holiday celebrations, and birthday parties are all special childhood events that kids with diabetes can still enjoy. Here are some tips to help make these celebrations a little easier.

- Plan ahead for special events so that treats fit into the meal plan.

- Talk to your doctor or diabetes educator about taking extra insulin to cover additional carbohydrate in treats. If your child uses an insulin pump, bolus before the treat as advised by your healthcare team.

- Include some activity time in kids' parties, preferably after a meal or snack. The extra activity will help the body to use up the extra carbohydrate and keep blood sugars in control.

- Offer alternatives to candy or other sweets. Examples include sugarless gum, stickers, crayons, or other small party favors.

- Provide nutritious snack choices like veggies and dip, apple slices, celery with peanut butter and raisins, pretzels, popcorn, party mix, or cheese cubes.

- Offer to bring treats for a school party or other special event. You know what your child is going to eat, and this provides an opportunity for all the kids to have a healthier snack.

- Develop new family traditions that focus on something other than food.

Diabetes Q&A

How do I know what a portion Is?

- A fruit serving is a small to medium piece, about the size of a tennis ball or 1/2 cup cut up.

- Vegetables are 1 cup raw leafy greens or 1/2 cup cooked.

- Meat is usually 3 ounces after cooking, or the size of a deck of cards without bone.

- Milk/yogurt is 1 cup or 8 ounces, low-fat or nonfat. Cheese is 1 ounce, or the size of your thumb length.

- Bread is 1 slice or 1/2 of a sandwich bun.

- Fat is 1 teaspoon of oil or margarine, about the size of the tip of your thumb, or 1 tablespoon of salad dressing, about the size of two thumbs together.

How does honey fit into a diabetic diet?

Both honey and sugar are carbohydrates and provide about the same amount of carbohydrate per tablespoon: honey has 16 grams of carbohydrate and 64 calories; white sugar has 12 grams and 48 calories; brown sugar has 13 grams and 52 calories. We average them all as 15 grams of carbohydrate, along with foods such as regular jelly or pancake syrup (1 tablespoon). Studies have shown honey's health benefits due to antioxidants and bacteria-fighting properties, but its effect on blood glucose is not consistently any better than sugar.

1 carbohydrate choice

= 15 grams of

carbohydrate, such as:

Fresh fruit	1 small piece
Canned fruit (light)	1/2 cup
Melon	1 cup
Berries	1 cup
Applesauce	1/2 cup
Banana	1/2
Popcorn	3 cups
Graham crackers	3 two-inch squares
Animal crackers	8
Pretzel sticks (thin)	45
Saltine crackers	6
Oyster crackers	60
Ice cream	1/2 cup
Gingersnaps	3
Vanilla wafers	5
Muffin	1 small
Cake doughnut (plain)	1
Sugar-free pudding	1/2 cup
Trail mix	1/2 cup

Nutrition

I thought sweets would raise my blood sugar more than starches. What has changed?
More recent research shows that sucrose (sugar) as part of a healthy diet does not necessarily raise blood sugar faster or higher than an equal amount of carbohydrate from bread and potatoes. However, it should be used in small amounts due to its low nutritional value and high calories. It is better to choose starchy foods that have fiber to slow their conversion to blood glucose. Portions of sweets are small for the amount of carbohydrate. A two-inch unfrosted brownie, for example, has the same carbohydrate as a full slice of whole wheat bread, and the brownie has more fat.

How much carbohydrate should I eat at each meal?
Carbohydrate needs are different for each person, and a meal plan should be worked out with a registered dietitian. However, a general guideline is about 45 to 60 grams per meal, more for an active man (about 75 to 90 grams), and less for a woman trying to lose weight (about 30 to 45 grams). Carbohydrate choices are carbohydrate foods that contain about 15 grams of carbohydrate each. Carbohydrate foods include bread and starchy vegetables, fruit, milk, sweets, and combination foods such as casseroles that have a starch, meat, and fat.

What about "net carbs" or "impact carbs"?
To get "net carbs," the manufacturer subtracts the fiber and the sugar alcohols to get low net carbs. For diabetes, you can subtract the fiber, but only subtract half the sugar alcohol grams. In general, it is wise to limit portions of these types of foods since they may have a laxative effect due to the sugar alcohols and may be high in calories.

What is the glycemic index and how should I use it?

The glycemic index (GI) is a ranking of carbohydrate foods based on how quickly portions with the same amount of carbohydrate are digested and converted to glucose to raise blood sugar. The GI value of a food has a ranking between 0 and 100, in comparison to pure glucose, the fastest carbohydrate, which has a value of 100. Examples of high GI foods, which would tend to cause a faster rise in blood sugar, include white bread, rice cakes, bagels, doughnuts, cornflakes, white rice, instant potatoes, ripe bananas, and pineapple. Low GI foods, which would act more slowly, include dried beans or legumes, nuts, whole grain breads, bran cereals, old-fashioned oats, barley, pasta (especially whole wheat), fresh fruit such as cherries, peaches, and grapefruit, milk, yogurt, soy milk, and green vegetables. A mixed meal with meat and fats may change how the carbohydrate is absorbed. Testing your blood sugar two hours after eating different food combinations is helpful in learning your own personal GI. Portion size and total carbohydrates still need to be considered when choosing lower glycemic index foods. Just because a food has a low GI doesn't make it a FREE food.

Some of my favorite foods have a high GI. Is there anything I can add to make the GI lower?

Adding vinegar or a healthy fat like olive oil can bring down the glycemic index. Have a low GI food like yogurt with a higher one like pineapple, for example. Other things that affect the impact on your blood sugar are the ripeness, cooking time, fiber and fat content, time of day eaten, and recent exercise. Cooking and processing a food raises its GI, which is why rice and corn cereals have a higher GI than old-fashioned oats, which are minimally processed. Cooking pasta until it is just done, or al dente, improves its GI. Preparing more foods with intact fibers, such as dried beans and grains like brown rice, results in slower digestion, so these foods have a lower GI. Oats and apples contain soluble fiber, which also slows digestion to lower their GI. You can use high GI foods when you need to treat a low blood sugar, but use the lower GI foods to smooth out the post-meal blood sugar.

Nutritional Profile Guidelines

The editors have attempted to present these family recipes in a format that allows approximate nutritional values to be computed. Persons with dietary or health problems or whose diets require close monitoring should not rely solely on the nutritional information provided. They should consult their physician or a registered dietitian for specific information.

Abbreviations for Nutritional Profile

CAL—Calories

PROT—Protein

CARBO—Carbohydrates

T FAT—Total Fat

SAT. FAT—Saturated Fat

MONOUFA—
    Monounsaturated Fatty Acids

FIBER—Dietary Fiber

SOD—Sodium

OMEGA-3 FA—
    Omega-3 Fatty Acids

K—Potassium

G—grams

MG—milligrams

Nutritional information for these recipes is computed from information derived from many sources, including materials supplied by the United States Department of Agriculture, computer databanks, and journals in which the information is assumed to be in the public domain. However, many specialty items, new products, and processed foods may not be available from these sources or may vary from the average values used in these profiles. More information on new and/or specific products may be obtained by reading the nutrient labels. Unless otherwise specified, the nutritional profile of these recipes is based on all measurements being level.

- Artificial sweeteners vary in use and strength and should be used to taste, using the recipe ingredients as a guideline. Sweeteners using aspartame (NutraSweet and Equal) should not be used as sweeteners in recipes involving prolonged heating, which reduces the sweet taste. For further information on the use of these sweeteners, refer to the package.

- Alcoholic ingredients have been analyzed for the basic information. Cooking causes the evaporation of alcohol, which decreases alcoholic and caloric content.

- Buttermilk, sour cream, and yogurt are the types available commercially.

- Canned beans and vegetables have been analyzed with the canning liquid. Rinsing and draining canned products will lower the sodium content.

- Chicken, cooked for boning and chopping, has been roasted; this method yields the lowest caloric values.

- Eggs are large Omega-3-enhanced. To avoid raw eggs that may carry salmonella, as in eggnog or six-week muffin batter, use eggs pasteurized in their shells, which are sold at some specialty food stores, or use an equivalent amount of pasteurized egg substitute.

- Flour is unsifted all-purpose flour.

- Garnishes, serving suggestions, and other optional information are not included in the profile.

- Margarine and butter are regular, not whipped or presoftened.

- Oil is either canola or olive.

- Salt and other ingredients to taste as noted in the ingredients have not been included in the nutritional profile.

- If a choice of ingredients has been given, the profile reflects the first option. If a choice of amounts has been given, the profile reflects the greater amount.

appetizers soups and salads

APPETIZER comes from the Latin APPETITUS,

meaning "strong desire." After you try these

recipes, you're sure to have a strong desire

to serve them again and again. The soups

and salads provide a tasty, nutritious start

to any meal.

Your body needs some fats in order to absorb the healthy carotenoids from fruits and vegetables. Research suggests that the "heart-healthy" fat found in avocados increases the body's ability to absorb and use carotenoids. Avocados are also rich in monounsaturated fats and Omega-3 fatty acids, which are the "good fats" that can help protect against heart disease.

Guacamole-with-a-Kick

1/2	**cup low-fat plain yogurt**
2	**small jalapeño chiles**
3	**Roma tomatoes, finely chopped**
1/2	**cup finely chopped white onion**
2	**tablespoons minced fresh cilantro**

1/2	**cup nonfat sour cream**
2	**large avocados**
2	**tablespoons fresh lime juice**
3	**ounces baked tortilla chips**

Line a strainer with cheesecloth, a coffee filter or a paper towel and set over a medium bowl; the strainer should not touch the bottom of the bowl. Spoon the yogurt into the prepared strainer and chill, covered, for 8 to 10 hours or until the yogurt cheese is thick and creamy.

Using a melon baller remove the seeds and ribs from the jalapeño chiles and mince the chiles. Mix the jalapeño chiles, tomatoes, onion and cilantro in a large bowl. Fold in the yogurt cheese and sour cream.

Peel the avocados, discard the pits and place in a bowl. Mash the avocados with a potato masher until smooth and drizzle with the lime juice. Immediately fold the avocado mixture into the tomato mixture. Serve with the tortilla chips.

NUTRIENTS PER SERVING   **Yield: 16 (3-tablespoon) servings**

CAL	PROT	CARBO	T FAT	SAT. FAT	MONOUFA	FIBER	SOD	OMEGA-3 FA	K
89	2G	10G	5G	1G	3G	2G	15MG	‹1G	259MG

PER SERVING	CARB CHOICES	1/2	CARB SOURCES				

Texas Caviar

1 (16-ounce) can black-eyed peas, drained and rinsed

3 tablespoons minced roasted red bell pepper

1 small tomato, finely chopped

1 jalapeño chile, seeded (optional) and minced

1 1/2 tablespoons chopped fresh parsley

1 tablespoon extra-virgin olive oil

1 teaspoon Worcestershire sauce

1 teaspoon balsamic vinegar

1/2 teaspoon chopped fresh oregano

1/8 teaspoon hot red pepper sauce

1/8 teaspoon coarse salt

Pepper to taste

Balsamic vinegar to taste

Toss the black-eyed peas, roasted bell pepper, tomato, jalapeño chile, parsley, olive oil, Worcestershire sauce, 1 teaspoon vinegar, the oregano and hot sauce in a bowl. Season with the salt and pepper. Drizzle with additional vinegar just before serving. Serve with a slotted spoon.

NUTRIENTS PER SERVING   **Yield: 4 servings**

CAL	PROT	CARBO	T FAT	SAT. FAT	MONOUFA	FIBER	SOD	OMEGA-3 FA	K
136	6G	19G	4G	1G	3G	4G	499MG	‹1G	271MG

PER SERVING	CARB CHOICES	1	CARB SOURCES				

Satay Beef Kabobs

Many name brands of peanut butter contain almost ZERO trans fat. Check the label.

Beef Kabobs

2	garlic cloves, minced
1/4	cup low-sodium soy sauce
1	tablespoon toasted sesame oil
1	teaspoon light brown sugar
1/2	teaspoon cumin
1/8	teaspoon crushed red pepper
1	pound boneless rib-eye roast
	Coarse salt and freshly ground black pepper to taste

Peanut Butter Sauce

1	tablespoon canola oil
1	garlic clove, minced
1/4	cup water
1/4	cup smooth peanut butter
1	teaspoon low-sodium soy sauce
1/2	teaspoon ketchup
1/4	teaspoon rice vinegar

For the kabobs, mix the garlic, soy sauce, sesame oil, brown sugar, cumin and red pepper in a bowl. Slice the beef against the grain into thirty-two 3x1x1/4-inch strips. Thread 2 slices of the beef onto each of 16 skewers and arrange the skewers in a shallow dish. Pour the soy sauce mixture over the beef. Marinate, covered, in the refrigerator for 45 minutes or preferably overnight, turning once.

Drain the beef, discarding the marinade. Season to taste with salt and black pepper. Grill the kabobs over high heat for 1 to 2 minutes per side for medium. Remove to a serving platter and cover to keep warm.

For the sauce, heat the canola oil in a small saucepan over medium heat. Stir in the garlic and cook for 3 minutes or until tender. Add the water and bring to a boil. Remove from the heat and whisk in the peanut butter, soy sauce, ketchup and vinegar until blended. Serve as a dipping sauce with the warm kabobs.

Nutritional profile includes the entire amount of the marinade.

NUTRIENTS PER KABOB — Yield: 16 kabobs

CAL	PROT	CARBO	T FAT	SAT. FAT	MONOUFA	FIBER	SOD	OMEGA-3 FA	K
85	6G	2G	6G	2G	3G	<1G	139MG	<1G	102MG

PER SERVING	CARB CHOICES	0	CARB SOURCES				

Rice Paper Spring Rolls

1	cup thinly sliced napa cabbage	1	teaspoon chopped fresh cilantro
1	cup bean sprouts	1	teaspoon minced garlic
1/2	cup peeled grated carrots	1/2	teaspoon grated fresh ginger
1/2	cup finely chopped cooked chicken	1	tablespoon Asian fish sauce
2	scallions, minced	1	tablespoon low-sodium soy sauce
2	tablespoons sesame seeds, toasted	1	teaspoon Tabasco sauce
1	teaspoon chopped fresh basil	1	teaspoon sesame oil
1	teaspoon chopped fresh mint	10	rice paper wrappers

Steam the cabbage for 1 minute; drain. Combine the cabbage, bean sprouts, carrots, chicken, scallions, sesame seeds, basil, mint, cilantro, garlic and ginger in a bowl and mix well. Stir in the fish sauce, soy sauce, Tabasco sauce and sesame oil.

Moisten the wrappers 1 or 2 at a time in warm water for 10 seconds and place on a clean tea towel. Spoon some of the cabbage mixture in the center of each wrapper and roll tucking in the edges so that the filling is completely enclosed. Chill, covered, until serving time. Serve with low-sodium soy sauce, if desired.

Taking a multivitamin every day can help ensure an adequate supply of healthy nutrients, since nutrient absorption may decrease with age or the use of certain medications.

NUTRIENTS PER SPRING ROLL   **Yield: 10 spring rolls**

CAL	PROT	CARBO	T FAT	SAT. FAT	MONOUFA	FIBER	SOD	OMEGA-3 FA	K
74	4G	10G	2G	‹1G	1G	1G	193MG	‹1G	93MG

PER SERVING	CARB CHOICES	1/2	CARB SOURCES					

Eggplant Caviar

2	eggplant	1/8	tablespoon coarse salt
1/4	cup fresh flat-leaf parsley leaves	1/8	tablespoon freshly ground pepper
1	tablespoon extra-virgin olive oil	1	whole grain baguette, sliced and toasted
1	garlic clove		
3/4	teaspoon allspice		

Make 2 or 3 slits in 1 side of each eggplant. Arrange the eggplant directly on the middle oven rack slit side up. Roast at 500 degrees for 20 minutes or until the eggplant are tender. The roasted eggplant will resemble flat tires at the end of the roasting process.

Peel the eggplant over a bowl using a sharp knife to reserve any juices and discard the peel. Place the eggplant and reserved juices in a food processor along with the parsley, olive oil, garlic, allspice, salt and pepper. Pulse to a paste consistency and spoon into a serving bowl. Surround the bowl with the toasted baguette slices.

NUTRIENTS PER SERVING   Yield: 4 servings

CAL	PROT	CARBO	T FAT	SAT. FAT	MONOUFA	FIBER	SOD	OMEGA-3 FA	K
113	3G	19G	4G	1G	3G	8G	245MG	<1G	550MG

PER SERVING	CARB CHOICES	1	CARB SOURCES				

Spicy Chicken Fingers

Chicken Fingers

4	(4-ounce) boneless skinless chicken breasts
1/2	teaspoon celery salt
1/8	teaspoon garlic powder
2	tablespoons red wine vinegar
2	teaspoons butter
1/4	teaspoon ground red pepper

Blue Cheese Sauce

1/4	cup nonfat sour cream
1/4	cup crumbled blue cheese
1	tablespoon Worcestershire sauce
1	tablespoon nonfat mayonnaise
1/2	teaspoon celery salt
1/8	teaspoon garlic powder

For the chicken fingers, cut the chicken into sixteen 1×4-inch fingers. Mix the celery salt and garlic powder in a small bowl and sprinkle over the chicken. Coat a large nonstick skillet with nonstick cooking spray and heat over medium-high heat.

Panfry the chicken in the hot skillet for 2 minutes per side. Remove from the heat and stir in the vinegar, butter and red pepper. Toss with a spatula to coat the chicken evenly. Remove the chicken to a serving platter and cover to keep warm.

For the sauce, mix the sour cream, blue cheese, Worcestershire sauce, mayonnaise, celery salt and garlic powder in a bowl. Serve as a dipping sauce with the chicken fingers.

NUTRIENTS PER SERVING   **Yield: 4 servings**

CAL	PROT	CARBO	T FAT	SAT. FAT	MONOUFA	FIBER	SOD	OMEGA-3 FA	K
192	26G	5G	7G	4G	2G	0G	622MG	‹1G	286MG

PER SERVING	CARB CHOICES	0	CARB SOURCES				

There is evidence that processed carbohydrates raise levels of the blood fat called triglycerides, which is often elevated in people with insulin resistance and diabetes. Substitute whole grains such as old-fashioned oatmeal, pumpernickel, or 12-grain bread for the morning breakfast roll.

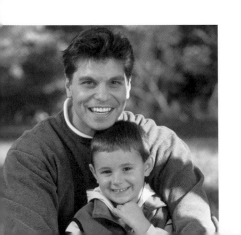

Focaccia Three Ways

**1   recipe Rosemary Focaccia
(page 115)**

Prepare the Rosemary Focaccia as directed omitting the rosemary and 1/2 teaspoon salt and substituting 1 of the following toppings:

1. Sprinkle with 3 slices crumbled cooked turkey bacon, 1/2 thinly sliced onion, 1/4 cup (1 ounce) shredded Cheddar cheese and pepper to taste

2. Top with 6 split asparagus spears diagonally cut into 1/2-inch pieces, 3 minced garlic cloves and 2 tablespoons fresh thyme leaves

3. Gently press 2 tablespoons chopped green olives and 2 tablespoons chopped black olives into the dough and sprinkle with 1 tablespoon minced fresh thyme or rosemary.

NUTRIENTS PER PIECE FOR 1.   Yield: 4 dozen bite-size pieces

CAL	PROT	CARBO	T FAT	SAT. FAT	MONOUFA	FIBER	SOD	OMEGA-3 FA	K
83	2G	12G	3G	1G	2G	1G	135MG	<1G	25MG

PER SERVING	CARB CHOICES	1	CARB SOURCES				

NUTRIENTS PER PIECE FOR 2.   Yield: 4 dozen bite-size pieces

CAL	PROT	CARBO	T FAT	SAT. FAT	MONOUFA	FIBER	SOD	OMEGA-3 FA	K
80	2G	12G	3G	<1G	2G	1G	121MG	<1G	28MG

PER SERVING	CARB CHOICES	1	CARB SOURCES				

NUTRIENTS PER PIECE FOR 3.   Yield: 4 dozen bite-size pieces

CAL	PROT	CARBO	T FAT	SAT. FAT	MONOUFA	FIBER	SOD	OMEGA-3 FA	K
80	2G	12G	3G	<1G	2G	1G	134MG	<1G	23MG

PER SERVING	CARB CHOICES	1	CARB SOURCES				

Crab-Stuffed Mushrooms

40	fresh mushrooms	1	rib celery, chopped
1	tablespoon butter	1/2	teaspoon coarse salt
1 1/2	pounds cooked crab meat, drained and shells removed	1/2	teaspoon freshly ground pepper
1/4	cup chopped fresh parsley	2	tablespoons chopped fresh parsley

Remove the stems from the mushrooms and finely chop the stems. Sauté the caps in the butter in a skillet. Remove to a bowl using a slotted spoon, reserving the pan drippings. Let stand until cool. Sauté the stems in the reserved pan drippings until tender and drain. Let stand until cool.

Combine the sautéed stems, crab meat, 1/4 cup parsley and celery in a bowl and mix gently. Season with the salt and pepper. Spoon the crab meat mixture into the caps on a serving platter. Sprinkle with 2 tablespoons parsley. Serve chilled or heat in a 140-degree oven until warm.

NUTRIENTS PER MUSHROOM   **Yield: 40 stuffed mushrooms**

CAL	PROT	CARBO	T FAT	SAT. FAT	MONOUFA	FIBER	SOD	OMEGA-3 FA	K
27	5G	1G	‹1G	‹1G	‹1G	‹1G	90MG	0G	140MG

PER SERVING	CARB CHOICES	0	CARB SOURCES				

Bay leaves are often used in soup, rice, and beef dishes. Western bay leaves are similar and can be substituted. Remove from the dish before serving, as a bay leaf can easily cut the mouth.

Black Bean and Corn Soup

3	**(15-ounce) cans low-sodium vegetable broth or chicken broth**
2	**(15-ounce) cans black beans, drained and rinsed**
1	**cup chopped onion**
1	**cup chopped celery**
2	**tablespoons olive oil**
2	**cups frozen corn**

1	**bay leaf**
2	**garlic cloves, minced**
1	**teaspoon oregano**
1/2	**teaspoon freshly ground pepper**
3	**tablespoons fresh lemon juice**
	Lemon slices
	Yogurt or sour cream to taste

Mix the broth and beans in a saucepan and bring to a boil. Reduce the heat to low and simmer for 5 minutes. Sauté the onion and celery in the olive oil in a skillet for 3 to 5 minutes or until tender-crisp. Stir the onion mixture, corn, bay leaf, garlic, oregano and pepper into the bean mixture and simmer, covered, for 45 minutes or until the vegetables are tender, stirring occasionally.

Discard the bay leaf and stir the lemon juice into the soup just before serving. The fresh lemon juice is the key to a great, not merely good, black bean soup. Ladle the soup into bowls and garnish with lemon slices and yogurt.

NUTRIENTS PER SERVING

Yield: 6 servings

CAL	PROT	CARBO	T FAT	SAT. FAT	MONOUFA	FIBER	SOD	OMEGA-3 FA	K
204	8G	41G	7G	1G	3G	10G	817MG	<1G	598MG

PER SERVING	CARB CHOICES	3	CARB SOURCES				

Tuscan Bread Soup

6   ounces country bread, torn into 1-inch pieces (3 cups)

3   carrots

2   tablespoons olive oil

1/2   large onion, cut into 1/4-inch pieces

2   ribs celery, cut into 1/4-inch slices

4   garlic cloves, crushed

1/8   teaspoon coarse salt

1/8   teaspoon freshly ground pepper

3   tablespoons tomato paste

1/4   head green cabbage, cut into quarters and thinly sliced (2 cups)

2   (14-ounce) cans reduced-sodium chicken broth

2   cups water

  Salt and pepper to taste

1/2   cup fresh parsley leaves

Spread the bread in a single layer on a baking sheet with sides. Toast at 500 degrees for 15 minutes or until the bread is dry, turning occasionally. Cut the carrots lengthwise into halves and cut each half into 1/4-inch slices.

Heat the olive oil in a medium saucepan over medium-high heat and add the carrots, onion, celery, garlic, 1/8 teaspoon salt and 1/8 teaspoon pepper. Cook for 8 to 10 minutes or until the vegetables are tender, stirring occasionally. Stir in the tomato paste.

Cook for 1 minute, stirring constantly. Add the toasted bread, cabbage, broth and water and mix well. Simmer over medium heat for 15 to 20 minutes or until thickened, stirring occasionally. Season to taste with salt and pepper and stir in the parsley. Ladle into soup bowls.

Freeze leftover soup in individual microwavable plastic containers for quick meals and snacks.

NUTRIENTS PER SERVING   Yield: 4 servings

CAL	PROT	CARBO	T FAT	SAT. FAT	MONOUFA	FIBER	SOD	OMEGA-3 FA	K
265	9G	38G	9G	1G	5G	5G	977MG	<1G	761MG

PER SERVING	CARB CHOICES	2 1/2	CARB SOURCES				

Minestrone

1	zucchini	1	(14-ounce) can diced tomatoes
1	tablespoon extra-virgin olive oil	6	cups (about) water
1/2	onion, chopped	1/8	teaspoon coarse salt
1	carrot, cut into 1/4-inch slices		Freshly ground pepper to taste
3	garlic cloves, minced	1	(19-ounce) can kidney beans, drained and rinsed
1/4	small head cabbage, cut lengthwise into halves and shredded	4	ounces small elbow macaroni
			Salt to taste
1	tablespoon chopped fresh rosemary, or 1 teaspoon dried rosemary	1/4	cup (1 ounce) grated Parmesan cheese

Cut the zucchini lengthwise into quarters and slice crosswise into 1/2-inch pieces. Heat the olive oil in a 6- to 8-quart stockpot over medium heat and add the onion, carrot and garlic. Cook for 3 to 4 minutes or until the onion is tender, stirring frequently. Stir in the zucchini, cabbage and rosemary.

Cook for 1 to 2 minutes or until the vegetables are coated, stirring constantly. Add the undrained tomatoes and enough water to cover the vegetables by 1 inch. Bring to a boil and reduce the heat to low. Stir in 1/8 teaspoon salt and pepper to taste.

Simmer for 10 minutes or until thickened, stirring occasionally. Stir in the beans and pasta and cook for 10 to 15 minutes longer or until the pasta is al dente, stirring occasionally. Season to taste with salt and pepper. Ladle into soup bowls and sprinkle with the cheese.

NUTRIENTS PER SERVING — Yield: 6 servings

CAL	PROT	CARBO	T FAT	SAT. FAT	MONOUFA	FIBER	SOD	OMEGA-3 FA	K
216	10G	36G	4G	1G	2G	7G	461MG	‹1G	460MG

PER SERVING	CARB CHOICES	2 1/2	CARB SOURCES				

One Great Gumbo

2	cups basmati rice
2	tablespoons extra-virgin olive oil
12	ounces chicken breasts, chopped
12	ounces boneless skinless chicken thighs, chopped
2	teaspoons poultry seasoning
1	pound turkey kielbasa, chopped
2	tablespoons butter
3	ribs celery (from heart of bunch), chopped
2	green bell peppers, chopped
1	large onion, chopped

2	fresh or dried bay leaves
2	tablespoons cayenne pepper sauce
2	tablespoons all-purpose flour
1	quart chicken stock or broth
2	cups chopped fresh or thawed frozen okra
1	(14-ounce) can each crushed sodium-free tomatoes and diced sodium-free tomatoes
2	to 3 tablespoons chopped fresh thyme leaves
5	scallions, thinly sliced diagonally

Prepare the rice using package directions. Remove from the heat and cover to keep warm. Preheat a heavy stockpot over medium-high heat. Add the olive oil to the hot stockpot and swirl to coat the bottom. Stir in the chicken and poultry seasoning and cook for 2 to 3 minutes or until brown on all sides, stirring frequently. Stir in the kielbasa and cook for 1 to 2 minutes longer. Remove the chicken and kielbasa to a bowl using a slotted spoon, reserving the pan drippings.

Add the butter to the reserved pan drippings and heat until melted. Stir in the celery, bell peppers, onion, bay leaves and pepper sauce. Cook for 3 to 5 minutes or until the vegetables begin to soften, stirring frequently. Mix in the flour and cook for 2 minutes, stirring constantly. Gradually stir in the stock and bring to a boil. Stir in the okra, chicken and kielbasa. Add the undrained tomatoes and 1/2 of the thyme and mix well. Bring to a boil and reduce the heat. Simmer for 5 minutes and discard the bay leaves. Ladle into soup bowls. Scoop the rice evenly into the center of each bowl using an ice cream scoop. Adding the rice on top of the gumbo will keep it from getting too soggy. Sprinkle with the remaining thyme and the scallions.

NUTRIENTS PER SERVING   Yield: 10 servings

CAL	PROT	CARBO	T FAT	SAT. FAT	MONOUFA	FIBER	SOD	OMEGA-3 FA	K
307	22G	29G	11G	4G	5G	3G	537MG	<1G	548MG

PER SERVING	CARB CHOICES	2	CARB SOURCES				

39

Chicken and Asparagus Salad

Lemon Dill Vinaigrette

1/4	cup olive oil
3	tablespoons balsamic vinegar
3	tablespoon rice vinegar
2	tablespoons white wine
2	tablespoons chopped fresh dill weed
2	tablespoons fresh lemon juice
1	large shallot, minced
2	garlic cloves, minced
1/4	teaspoon salt, or to taste

Salad

12	small red potatoes, cut into halves
6	(5-ounce) boneless skinless chicken breasts
	Salt to taste
1/2	teaspoon freshly ground pepper
1/4	cup white wine
1	tablespoon minced fresh basil
1	tablespoon minced fresh parsley
1	bunch fresh asparagus
2	cups mixed baby greens
6	radishes, cut into rosettes

For the vinaigrette, combine the olive oil, balsamic vinegar, rice vinegar, wine, dill weed, lemon juice, shallot, garlic and salt in a bowl and whisk until combined.

For the salad, add enough water to a saucepan to measure approximately 2 inches and bring to a boil. Add the potatoes to the boiling water and cover. Steam for 30 minutes or until tender. Drain the potatoes and remove to a large bowl.

Arrange the chicken in a single layer in a baking dish and sprinkle with salt and pepper. Drizzle with the wine and sprinkle with the basil and parsley. Bake at 325 degrees for 30 minutes. Cut each chicken breast diagonally into 3 equal pieces.

Snap 2 inches off the bottom of each asparagus spear and blanch the spears in boiling water in a saucepan for 2 minutes or just until tender; drain. Cool to room temperature. Cut each spear lengthwise down the center.

Place 1/3 cup of the greens on a plate. Arrange 6 or 7 of the cut asparagus spears on top of the greens with the tips pointing outward, creating the impression of a fan. Arrange 3 pieces of the chicken between the fanned asparagus spears. Pour 1/2 of the vinaigrette over the potatoes and toss to coat.

Arrange 4 potato halves in the center of the asparagus arrangement and drizzle with 1 tablespoon of the remaining vinaigrette. Top with a radish rosette. Repeat the process with the remaining greens, remaining asparagus, remaining chicken, remaining potatoes, remaining vinaigrette and remaining radishes.

Blanch: Place food in cold water, bring to a boil for the time specified, drain, and plunge into cold water to stop the cooking process. This is often used to loosen the skin of tomatoes for easier peeling or to partially cook fresh vegetables for use in a recipe.

Nutritional profile includes the entire amount of the vinaigrette.

NUTRIENTS PER SERVING   **Yield: 6 servings**

CAL	PROT	CARBO	T FAT	SAT. FAT	MONOUFA	FIBER	SOD	OMEGA-3 FA	K
367	31G	30G	12G	2G	8G	4G	181MG	‹1G	1084MG

PER SERVING	CARB CHOICES	2	CARB SOURCES				

41

Mango Chicken Salad with Brown Rice

2	cups water	1	teaspoon grated fresh ginger
1	cup brown rice	1/4	teaspoon salt
6	ounces green beans, trimmed and cut into halves (about 2 cups)	1/2	cup minced scallions
12	ounces boneless skinless chicken breasts, cut into 1/2-inch strips	1	red bell pepper, cut into 1/4-inch strips
1	tablespoon low-sodium soy sauce	1	mango, peeled and cut into 1/4-inch pieces
1/4	cup rice wine vinegar	2	tablespoons chopped fresh cilantro
2	tablespoons canola oil		
1	teaspoon sesame oil		

Bring the water and brown rice to a boil in a saucepan. Reduce the heat to low and cook, covered, for 25 to 45 minutes or until the water is absorbed and the rice is tender. Remove the rice to a colander and rinse with cold water; drain.

Fill a small saucepan halfway with water and bring to a boil over high heat. Add the beans and cook for 3 minutes or until tender-crisp. Drain and rinse with cold water to stop the cooking process. Toss the chicken and soy sauce in a bowl until coated.

Lightly coat a nonstick skillet with nonstick cooking spray and heat over medium heat. Gradually add the chicken to the hot skillet and cook for 1 to 2 minutes per side or until evenly brown and cooked through, turning as needed. Remove the chicken to a bowl.

Whisk the vinegar, canola oil, sesame oil, ginger and salt in a large bowl. Add the rice, beans, chicken, scallions, bell pepper and 1/2 of the mango and gently toss to combine. Spoon the salad onto a serving platter and sprinkle with the cilantro. Top with the remaining mango.

NUTRIENTS PER SERVING   Yield: 4 servings

CAL	PROT	CARBO	T FAT	SAT. FAT	MONOUFA	FIBER	SOD	OMEGA-3 FA	K
402	22G	52G	12G	2G	5G	5G	292MG	1G	541MG

PER SERVING	CARB CHOICES	3 1/2	CARB SOURCES	

Turkey Wild Rice Salad

2³/₄ cups water	¹/₄ cup chopped fresh parsley
²/₃ cup wild rice	¹/₄ cup finely chopped purple onion
1¹/₄ cups chopped roasted lean turkey	2 tablespoons canola oil
¹/₂ cup minced celery	2 tablespoons sherry vinegar
¹/₂ cup drained canned mandarin oranges, cut into halves	1 tablespoon mandarin orange juice
¹/₂ cup dried cranberries	1 teaspoon Dijon mustard

Combine the water and wild rice in a medium saucepan and bring to a boil. Reduce the heat and simmer, covered, for 1 hour or until the liquid is absorbed and the rice is tender.

Combine the wild rice, turkey, celery, mandarin oranges, dried cranberries, parsley and onion in a bowl and mix well. Add a mixture of the canola oil, vinegar, juice and Dijon mustard to the rice mixture and toss to coat. Serve at room temperature.

What foods contain magnesium and how much do you need every day? Adult women need 280 milligrams and men need 350 milligrams. Peanut butter has 60 milligrams per tablespoon. Other sources include wild rice, wheat germ, bran cereals, lentils, baking cocoa, almonds, spinach, yogurt, milk, fish, and fortified breakfast cereals.

NUTRIENTS PER SERVING   **Yield: 4 (1-cup) servings**

CAL	PROT	CARBO	T FAT	SAT. FAT	MONOUFA	FIBER	SOD	OMEGA-3 FA	K
303	17G	39G	10G	1G	5G	3G	79MG	1G	375MG

PER SERVING	CARB CHOICES **2¹/2**	CARB SOURCES				

Check labels at the grocery story and choose low-sodium, reduced-salt, or no-salt-added products. This is especially true for soy sauce and tomato-based products, which can use up your sodium allowance for a day.

salads

Toasted Millet Salad with Salmon and Snow Peas

1	teaspoon canola oil		1	tablespoon sesame oil
1	cup millet		1	tablespoon low-sodium soy sauce
2 1/2	cups boiling water		2	teaspoons grated fresh ginger
8	ounces boneless skinless salmon fillets		1	teaspoon minced garlic
1	teaspoon low-sodium soy sauce		1/4	teaspoon salt
2	cups fresh snow peas, trimmed		2	tablespoons canola oil
1/2	cup rice wine vinegar		1/2	cup minced scallions
2	tablespoons water		1/2	cup finely chopped red bell pepper

Coat the bottom of a large sauté pan with 1 teaspoon canola oil. Add the millet to the prepared pan and cook over medium-low heat for 10 minutes or until fragrant, stirring constantly. Add the boiling water to the millet and mix well. Cook, covered, over medium-low heat for 25 minutes or until the water is absorbed and the millet is tender. Remove from the heat and let stand, uncovered, until cool.

Coat the salmon with 1 teaspoon soy sauce. Heat a large skillet over high heat and add the salmon. Reduce the heat to medium and cook for 3 minutes or until brown. Turn the salmon and cook for 3 to 5 minutes longer or until the salmon flakes easily. Cool in the pan and break into 1-inch cubes. Fill a small saucepan halfway with water and bring to a boil. Add the snow peas and cook for 1 minute; drain. Rinse with cold water and blot dry with paper towels.

Whisk the vinegar, 2 tablespoons water, the sesame oil, 1 tablespoon soy sauce, the ginger, garlic, salt and 2 tablespoons canola oil in a bowl. Add the vinegar mixture and salmon to the millet and toss gently to mix. Spoon the salad onto a serving platter and top with the snow peas, scallions and bell pepper.

NUTRIENTS PER SERVING   Yield: 4 servings

CAL	PROT	CARBO	T FAT	SAT. FAT	MONOUFA	FIBER	SOD	OMEGA-3 FA	K
435	20G	46G	19G	2G	8G	6G	314MG	1G	431MG

PER SERVING	CARB CHOICES	3	CARB SOURCES				

Shrimp Wild Rice Salad

Balsamic Dressing

1	cup olive oil
1/2	cup balsamic vinegar
1/4	cup honey
1/2	teaspoon dry mustard

Salad

1	pound shrimp
6	cups water
1	cup wild rice
1	cup long grain rice
1/2	cup chopped green bell pepper
1/2	cup chopped celery
1/2	cup chopped scallions
1/4	cup chopped fresh parsley

For the dressing, whisk the olive oil, vinegar, honey and dry mustard in a bowl until combined.

For the salad, add the shrimp to a large saucepan of boiling water and boil for 2 minutes or until the shrimp turn pink; drain. Cool slightly and peel and devein the shrimp. Bring 6 cups water to a boil in a saucepan and stir in the wild rice.

Cook, covered, over medium heat for 15 minutes. Stir in the long grain rice and reduce the heat to low. Simmer, covered, for 20 minutes. Remove from the heat and let stand, covered, for 10 minutes or longer; drain, if necessary. Add the bell pepper, celery, scallions, parsley and 3/4 cup of the dressing to the rice and mix well. Spoon the rice mixture onto a serving platter and arrange the shrimp in the center of the rice. Serve at room temperature.

Nutritional profile includes 2 tablespoons of the dressing per serving.

NUTRIENTS PER SERVING   **Yield: 6 servings**

CAL	PROT	CARBO	T FAT	SAT. FAT	MONOUFA	FIBER	SOD	OMEGA-3 FA	K
439	19G	54G	17G	2G	12G	3G	146MG	‹1G	348MG

PER SERVING	CARB CHOICES	3 1/2	CARB SOURCES	

To lower cholesterol, include in your diet foods high in fiber. Try a cereal such as Kellogg's Bran Buds, which contains psyllium, shown to lower LDL and total cholesterol, or Kashi brand cereals with soy and fiber. It also helps to include two to three servings per day of margarine spread containing plant sterols or stanols, such as Benecol, Take Control, or Smart Balance Omega Plus, in place of your regular butter or margarine.

Curried Barley and Shrimp Salad

3	cups water
1	teaspoon curry powder
1/2	teaspoon turmeric
1	cup barley
1	pound frozen, deveined, peeled and cooked small shrimp, thawed and drained
1 1/2	cups chopped seeded tomatoes
1/2	cup chopped green bell pepper
1/2	cup chopped peeled cucumber
5	tablespoons fresh lime juice

3	tablespoons canola oil
1	teaspoon finely chopped seeded jalapeño chile, or to taste
1	garlic clove, minced
1/4	teaspoon salt
	Romaine lettuce leaves or other green leafy lettuce
3	tablespoons chopped fresh basil or cilantro
1	lime, cut into quarters

Combine the water, curry powder and turmeric in a saucepan and bring to a boil. Stir in the barley. Cook, covered, over low heat for 45 minutes or until the water is absorbed and the barley is tender. Remove the barley to a colander and rinse with cold water; drain.

Combine the barley, shrimp, tomatoes, bell pepper and cucumber in a bowl and mix gently. Whisk the lime juice, canola oil, jalapeño chile, garlic and salt in a bowl until combined. Add the lime juice mixture to the barley mixture and toss to coat. Spoon the barley salad onto a lettuce-lined platter and sprinkle with the basil. Garnish with the lime quarters.

NUTRIENTS PER SERVING   Yield: 6 servings

CAL	PROT	CARBO	T FAT	SAT. FAT	MONOUFA	FIBER	SOD	OMEGA-3 FA	K
228	11G	30G	8G	1G	4G	6G	295MG	1G	260MG

PER SERVING	CARB CHOICES	2	CARB SOURCES				

Southwestern Salad

16	ounces whole wheat pasta
6	ripe tomatoes
1	teaspoon salt
3/4	teaspoon freshly ground pepper
1	cup frozen corn
1/2	cup roasted garlic

1/4	cup loosely packed fresh basil leaves, finely chopped or torn
1/2	to 3/4 cup olive oil
1/2	cup (2 ounces) grated Parmesan cheese

Cook the pasta in boiling water in a saucepan until tender but slightly chewy; drain. Cut the tomatoes into bite-size pieces. Place in a bowl and sprinkle with the salt and pepper. Stir and let stand for 15 minutes to allow the juices to seep out of the tomatoes; drain.

Microwave the corn in a microwave-safe dish for 1 minute. Mix the drained tomatoes, corn, roasted garlic, basil and olive oil in a bowl. Add the pasta and toss to combine. Stir in the cheese. Serve at room temperature.

NUTRIENTS PER SERVING   Yield: 6 servings

CAL	PROT	CARBO	T FAT	SAT. FAT	MONOUFA	FIBER	SOD	OMEGA-3 FA	K
611	18G	74G	31G	5G	21G	14G	508MG	<1G	627MG

PER SERVING	CARB CHOICES	5	CARB SOURCES				

If you would like to try to lower your blood sugar response to potatoes, precook them and eat them cold as in potato salad or reheated. They have a lower effect on after-meal blood sugar compared to those same potatoes cooked and eaten immediately. When the starch in potatoes cools, it forms a resistant starch that delays digestion and absorption.

Dijon Potato Salad

Buttermilk Dressing

1/2 **cup buttermilk**

2 **tablespoons low-fat mayonnaise**

1 **tablespoon Dijon mustard**

1 **tablespoon tarragon vinegar**

Salad

1 **pound unpeeled red potatoes, coarsely chopped**

1/2 **cup diagonally sliced celery**

1/4 **cup sliced scallions**

2 **tablespoons chopped shallots**

For the dressing, combine the buttermilk, mayonnaise, Dijon mustard and vinegar in bowl and mix well. Chill in the refrigerator.

For the salad, combine the potatoes with enough water to cover in a saucepan. Bring to a boil and reduce the heat to medium. Cook for 15 minutes or until the potatoes are tender but firm; drain. Toss the potatoes with the celery, scallions and shallots in a bowl. Add the dressing and mix well. Chill, covered, until serving time.

NUTRIENTS PER SERVING								Yield: 6 (1/2-cup) servings	
CAL	PROT	CARBO	T FAT	SAT. FAT	MONOUFA	FIBER	SOD	OMEGA-3 FA	K
88	3G	15G	2G	‹1G	‹1G	2G	138MG	‹1G	431MG

PER SERVING	CARB CHOICES	**1**	CARB SOURCES				

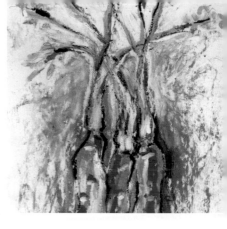

Stacked Vegetable Salad

4	slices turkey bacon	1	pint cherry tomatoes, cut into halves
8	ounces red potatoes, cut into 1/2-inch pieces	1	large red bell pepper, cut into thin strips
2	cups frozen corn kernels	2	cups nonfat mayonnaise
8	ounces baby carrots, cut lengthwise into halves	1	cup reduced-fat sour cream
1	(10-ounce) package frozen green peas	1/4	cup chopped fresh chives
6	ounces fresh snow peas (2 cups)	1/2	cup (2 ounces) shredded Cheddar cheese
2	cups shredded red cabbage		

Cook the bacon in a skillet until crisp; drain. Crumble the bacon and chill in the refrigerator. Combine the potatoes with enough water to cover in a large saucepan and bring to a boil. Cook for 5 minutes or until tender. Remove the potatoes to a colander using a slotted spoon, reserving the cooking liquid. Rinse the potatoes with cold water and drain.

Set out a large bowl of ice water. Blanch the corn and carrots separately in the reserved cooking liquid for 3 minutes each. Immediately plunge the vegetables separately into the ice water. Remove with a slotted spoon to a double layer of paper towels to drain, reserving the cooking liquid. Blanch the green peas and snow peas separately in the reserved cooking liquid for 2 minutes each. Immediately plunge the vegetables separately into the ice water. Remove with a slotted spoon to the paper towels to drain. Discard the cooking liquid.

Layer the cabbage, green peas, tomatoes, potatoes, carrots, snow peas, corn and bell pepper in a straight-sided 6-quart glass bowl or a 9x13-inch dish. Mix the mayonnaise, sour cream and chives in a bowl and spread over the top of the layers. Chill, covered, for up to 4 hours. Sprinkle with the cheese, bacon and additional chives before serving.

NUTRIENTS PER SERVING									Yield: 12 servings
CAL	PROT	CARBO	T FAT	SAT. FAT	MONOUFA	FIBER	SOD	OMEGA-3 FA	K
168	6G	24G	5G	3G	1G	4G	428MG	<1G	428MG

PER SERVING	CARB CHOICES	1 1/2	CARB SOURCES				

entrées

Travel around the world through these

pages. You'll savor the influences of Asian,

Italian, Indian, Mexican, Greek, French,

and American cuisines in these delicious

main dishes.

Italian Pot Roast

1	(3-pound) beef chuck roast, trimmed and cut crosswise into halves	1	(28-ounce) can crushed tomatoes
5	garlic cloves, cut lengthwise into halves	1	pound small white unpeeled potatoes
1 1/2	teaspoons coarse salt	1	large onion, cut into 8 wedges
1	teaspoon pepper	1	tablespoon chopped fresh rosemary, or 1 teaspoon crumbled dried rosemary
1	tablespoon olive oil		

Cut 4 slits in the beef roast and stuff the slits with 1/2 of the garlic. Sprinkle with the salt and pepper. Heat the olive oil in a large skillet over high heat and swirl to coat the bottom of the skillet. Add the beef to the hot oil and cook for 5 minutes or until brown on all sides.

Combine the beef, undrained tomatoes, potatoes, onion, rosemary and remaining garlic in a 5-quart slow cooker. Cook, covered, on High for 6 hours or until the beef is fork tender; do not remove the cover during the cooking process. Remove the beef to a cutting board and thinly slice, discarding any gristle. Skim the fat from the top of the sauce. To serve, divide the beef and vegetables evenly among 8 bowls and drizzle with the sauce.

NUTRIENTS PER SERVING   Yield: 8 servings

CAL	PROT	CARBO	T FAT	SAT. FAT	MONOUFA	FIBER	SOD	OMEGA-3 FA	K
279	35G	16G	8G	3G	4G	2G	541MG	<1G	757MG

PER SERVING	CARB CHOICES	1	CARB SOURCES				

Peppercorn Sirloin with Cabernet Sauce

4	(4-ounce) sirloin steaks	1	tablespoon extra-virgin olive oil
1	teaspoon coarse salt	1	cup cabernet sauvignon
3	tablespoons freshly ground pepper	2	tablespoons butter

Pat the steaks dry with paper towels and sprinkle with the salt and pepper. Heat the olive oil in a large skillet over medium-high heat just to the smoking point. Carefully add the steaks to the hot oil and cook for 3 minutes. Turn the steaks and cook for 3 minutes longer or until deep brown in color for medium-rare. Remove the steaks to a platter and cover to keep warm.

Drain the pan drippings from the skillet and add the wine. Cook over medium heat for about 7 minutes or until the wine is reduced to 1/4 cup. Scrape the bottom of the skillet with a wooden spoon to dislodge any brown bits and whisk in the butter. Drizzle the sauce over the steaks and serve immediately.

NUTRIENTS PER SERVING   Yield: 4 servings

CAL	PROT	CARBO	T FAT	SAT. FAT	MONOUFA	FIBER	SOD	OMEGA-3 FA	K
285	25G	4G	14G	6G	6G	1G	535MG	<1G	379MG

PER SERVING	CARB CHOICES	0	CARB SOURCES				

Sirloin with Garden Vegetables

3	garlic cloves, minced	1	pound fresh green beans, trimmed
1/4	teaspoon pepper	3/4	cup thinly sliced red onion
1	(2¼-pound) bone-in beef sirloin steak, 1¼ inches thick	2	tablespoons white wine vinegar
		2	teaspoons extra-virgin olive oil
1	pound red potatoes, cut into quarters	1/4	teaspoon pepper
		1/4	teaspoon sugar

Mash the garlic and 1/4 teaspoon pepper on a cutting board with the side of a chef's knife until a chunky paste forms. Rub both sides of the steak with the garlic paste. Combine the potatoes with enough water to cover in a saucepan and bring to a boil.

Reduce the heat and simmer for 5 minutes. Add the beans and cook for 3 to 4 minutes longer or until the potatoes are tender and the beans are tender-crisp; drain. Rinse the vegetables with cool water and place in a large bowl. Rinse the onion in a colander with hot tap water and drain. Whisk the vinegar, olive oil, 1/4 teaspoon pepper and the sugar in a small bowl until combined.

Heat a large heavy ovenproof skillet over medium-high heat until hot but not smoking. Sear the steak in the hot skillet for 3 minutes on each side or until brown. Bake at 375 degrees for 15 to 18 minutes or until a meat thermometer registers 145 degrees for medium-rare or for 20 to 23 minutes or until a meat thermometer registers 160 degrees for medium. Let stand for 5 minutes.

Trim any remaining fat from the steak and thinly slice. Arrange the sliced steak on a serving platter and surround with the potatoes, beans and onion. Drizzle with the vinaigrette and serve immediately.

NUTRIENTS PER SERVING   Yield: 8 servings

CAL	PROT	CARBO	T FAT	SAT. FAT	MONOUFA	FIBER	SOD	OMEGA-3 FA	K
227	27G	15G	6G	2G	3G	3G	56MG	‹1G	746MG

PER SERVING	CARB CHOICES	1	CARB SOURCES				

Shiitake Mushroom and Beef Stir-Fry

1	(12-ounce) beef sirloin steak	3	tablespoons hoisin sauce
2	tablespoons low-sodium teriyaki sauce	2	tablespoons cornstarch
10	shiitake mushrooms, stems removed	3	teaspoons olive oil
		4	scallions, thinly sliced diagonally
8	ounces sugar snap peas or snow peas, ends trimmed	2	garlic cloves, crushed
1/4	cup low-sodium chicken broth	2	large red bell peppers, cut into strips
		1 1/4	cups low-sodium chicken broth

Freeze the steak for 20 minutes for easier slicing. Cut the steak across the grain into 1/2-inch-thick-strips. Cut the extra long strips crosswise into halves. Combine the steak with the teriyaki sauce in sealable plastic bag. Seal tightly and chill for 15 minutes to several hours, turning occasionally. Slice the mushroom caps. Remove the strings from the peas. Mix 1/4 cup broth and the hoisin sauce in a bowl. Whisk in the cornstarch until blended.

Heat 1 teaspoon of the olive oil in a large nonstick skillet or wok over high heat until hot but not smoking. Add the scallions and stir-fry for 1 minute. Remove the scallions with a slotted spoon to a bowl. Add the steak and garlic to the pan drippings and stir-fry for 2 minutes or until the steak is no longer pink. Remove the steak mixture to the bowl with a slotted spoon. Add 1 teaspoon of the remaining olive oil to the reserved pan drippings. Add the mushrooms and stir-fry for 3 minutes or until softened. Remove the mushrooms with a slotted spoon and add to the steak mixture. Add the remaining 1 teaspoon olive oil to the pan drippings. Stir-fry the peas and bell peppers in the olive oil mixture for 1 to 2 minutes or just until softened. Return the steak mixture to the skillet and stir in 1 1/4 cups broth.

Cook, covered, over medium heat for 2 to 3 minutes or just until heated through. Whisk the hoisin sauce mixture and add to the steak mixture. Stir-fry until the sauce begins to boil and cook for 1 minute longer.

NUTRIENTS PER SERVING · Yield: 4 servings

CAL	PROT	CARBO	T FAT	SAT. FAT	MONOUFA	FIBER	SOD	OMEGA-3 FA	K
260	24G	23G	8G	2G	4G	4G	400MG	<1G	685MG

PER SERVING	CARB CHOICES	1 1/2	CARB SOURCES		OTHER SOURCES	

Grilled Lamb Chops with Cherry Apple Relish

Cherry Apple Relish

1	green apple, cut into 1/2-inch pieces
1/4	cup dried cherries
1/4	cup apple juice, heated
1	tablespoon extra-virgin olive oil
1	tablespoon balsamic vinegar
1	teaspoon freshly ground pepper
1	teaspoon brown sugar
1/8	teaspoon coarse salt

Lamb

2	tablespoons extra-virgin olive oil
2	tablespoons finely chopped fresh rosemary leaves
4	(2 1/2-ounce) lamb loin chops
1	teaspoon coarse salt
4	teaspoons freshly ground pepper

For the relish, combine the apple, cherries, apple juice, olive oil, vinegar, pepper, brown sugar and salt in a bowl and mix well. Store, covered, in the refrigerator. The flavor is enhanced if prepared 1 day in advance.

For the lamb, combine the olive oil and rosemary in a shallow dish and add the lamb chops, turning to coat. Sprinkle with the salt and pepper. Chill, covered, for 1 hour. Grill the lamb chops over medium-hot coals for 20 minutes or to the desired degree of doneness. Serve with the relish.

NUTRIENTS PER SERVING   Yield: 4 servings

CAL	PROT	CARBO	T FAT	SAT. FAT	MONOUFA	FIBER	SOD	OMEGA-3 FA	K
256	14G	17G	15G	3G	10G	2G	579MG	<1G	228MG

PER SERVING	CARBO CHOICES	1	CARB SOURCES				

Grilled Cinnamon
Pork Tenderloin

2	(12-ounce) pork tenderloins	1¹/₂	teaspoons honey
3	tablespoons low-sodium soy sauce	2	garlic cloves, crushed
3	tablespoons cooking sherry	¹/₂	teaspoon cinnamon
1	tablespoon brown sugar		

Place the tenderloins in a large sealable plastic bag. Mix the soy sauce, sherry, brown sugar, honey, garlic and cinnamon in a bowl and pour over the tenderloins. Seal tightly and turn to coat. Marinate in the refrigerator for up to 6 hours, turning occasionally. The flavor of the tenderloin is lost if marinated longer.

Remove the tenderloins from the marinade and insert a meat thermometer in one of the tenderloins. Grill over hot coals for 15 minutes or until the thermometer registers 160 degrees for medium, turning occasionally.

Use a clean thermometer that measures the internal temperature of cooked food to ensure that meat, poultry, and casseroles are cooked to safe temperatures: Medium-rare beef, veal and lamb—145 degrees; Medium-well beef, egg dishes, ground meats and pork—160 degrees; Stuffing, ground poultry, and reheated leftovers—165 degrees; Poultry breasts—170 degrees whole—180 degrees.

Nutritional profile includes the entire amount of the marinade.

NUTRIENTS PER SERVING   **Yield: 6 servings**

CAL	PROT	CARBO	T FAT	SAT. FAT	MONOUFA	FIBER	SOD	OMEGA-3 FA	K
158	23G	5G	4G	1G	2G	‹1G	286MG	‹1G	384MG

PER SERVING	CARB CHOICES	1/2	CARB SOURCES				

Using olive oil in place of saturated fats helps to lower total cholesterol and LDL (bad) without lowering HDL (good). Besides olive oil, other good sources of fat are canola oil and margarine, peanuts, peanut oil and peanut butter, other nuts (except walnuts), olives, and avocados.

Crusted Herb Pork Chops

3	**tablespoons finely chopped fresh parsley**		**1**	**tablespoon extra-virgin olive oil**
3	**tablespoons finely chopped fresh rosemary**		**1**	**teaspoon coarse salt**
1¹/₂	**tablespoons finely chopped fresh sage**		**¹/₂**	**teaspoon freshly ground pepper**
			4	**(3-ounce) boneless pork loin chops**

Mix the parsley, rosemary, sage, olive oil, salt and pepper in a bowl. Coat the pork chops with the herb mixture. Arrange the pork chops on a grill rack and grill over medium-high heat for 3 to 5 minutes per side or until the herbs are deep brown in color.

Remove the pork chops to a heated platter and tent with foil. Let stand for 5 minutes before serving.

NUTRIENTS PER SERVING									Yield: 4 servings
CAL	PROT	CARBO	T FAT	SAT. FAT	MONOUFA	FIBER	SOD	OMEGA-3 FA	K
155	18G	1G	8G	2G	5G	‹1G	518MG	‹1G	251MG

PER SERVING	CARB CHOICES	0	CARB SOURCES				

Chicken Cassoulet

2	cups dried Great Northern beans or cannellini
8	ounces boneless skinless chicken thighs
2	carrots, cut into 1/2-inch pieces
1	red bell pepper or green bell pepper, cut into 1/2-inch pieces
1	cup chopped onion
4	garlic cloves, minced
1	(14-ounce) can low-sodium Italian-style stewed tomatoes
8	ounces fully cooked smoked lite turkey sausage, cut into halves lengthwise and cut into 1/2-inch slices
3	cups low-sodium chicken broth
1	cup dry white wine or low-sodium chicken broth
2	tablespoons snipped fresh parsley
2	teaspoons dried thyme, crushed
1/2	teaspoon ground red pepper
1	bay leaf

Sort and rinse the beans. Cook the beans in a saucepan using the package directions. Cut the chicken into 1-inch pieces.

Place the carrots, bell pepper, onion, garlic, cooked beans, undrained tomatoes, chicken and sausage in a 3 1/2- to 5-quart slow cooker. Combine the chicken broth, wine, parsley, thyme, red pepper and bay leaf in a bowl and mix well. Pour into the slow cooker. Cook, covered, on Low for 7 to 8 hours or on High for 3 1/2 to 4 hours. Discard the bay leaf before serving.

NUTRIENTS PER SERVING   **Yield: 6 servings**

CAL	PROT	CARBO	T FAT	SAT. FAT	MONOUFA	FIBER	SOD	OMEGA-3 FA	K
402	30G	48G	8G	2G	3G	13G	322MG	‹1G	1110MG

PER SERVING	CARB CHOICES	3	CARB SOURCES

When making a
sauce, reduce the
liquids in a large skillet.
The larger the surface
area, the more quickly
the liquid will evaporate.

entreés

Chicken with Sun-Dried Tomato Sauce

4	(6-ounce) boneless skinless chicken breasts		1/8	teaspoon hot red pepper flakes
	Salt and black pepper to taste		1/4	cup dry white wine
1	tablespoon olive oil		3/4	cup chicken broth
4	garlic cloves, minced		1/4	cup fat-free half-and-half
1/4	cup drained sun-dried tomatoes, patted dry and coarsely chopped		1/4	cup thinly sliced fresh basil leaves
				Salt and black pepper to taste

Pat the chicken dry with paper towels and sprinkle with salt and black pepper. Heat the olive oil in a 12-inch heavy skillet over medium-high heat until hot but not smoking. Brown the chicken in the hot oil for 6 minutes, turning once. The chicken will not be cooked through. Remove the chicken with tongs to a platter, reserving the pan drippings.

Sauté the garlic, tomatoes and red pepper flakes in the reserved pan drippings for 1 minute or until the garlic is pale golden in color. Stir in the wine and bring to a boil. Boil for 1 minute or until reduced by half, stirring constantly to dislodge any brown bits. Mix in the broth and cover. Bring to a boil and add the chicken and any accumulated juices.

Simmer, covered, for 4 to 5 minutes or just until the chicken is cooked through. Remove the chicken with tongs to a platter and cover loosely with foil to keep warm, reserving the sauce. Stir the half-and-half and 2 tablespoons of the basil into the reserved sauce and bring just to a simmer, stirring frequently. Season to taste with salt and black pepper. Drizzle the sauce over the chicken and sprinkle with the remaining 2 tablespoons basil. Serve immediately.

NUTRIENTS PER SERVING   Yield: 4 servings

CAL	PROT	CARBO	T FAT	SAT. FAT	MONOUFA	FIBER	SOD	OMEGA-3 FA	K
254	36G	4G	9G	2G	5G	1G	298MG	‹1G	458MG

PER SERVING	CARB CHOICES	0	CARB SOURCES				

Red Potato and Chicken Pizzaiola

1	tablespoon extra-virgin olive oil	2	teaspoons oregano
4	(4-ounce) boneless skinless chicken breasts	1/8	teaspoon red pepper flakes
1/4	teaspoon salt	1	(14-ounce) can Italian-style diced tomatoes
1/4	teaspoon black pepper	1	(14-ounce) can low-sodium chicken broth
1	pound new red potatoes, cut into quarters	3	tablespoons tomato paste
1	onion, chopped		
2	green bell peppers, cut into 1/2-inch strips		

Heat the olive oil in a large ovenproof skillet over medium heat. Season the chicken on both sides with the salt and black pepper. Sauté the chicken in the hot oil until brown on both sides. Remove the chicken to a platter using tongs and cover to keep warm, reserving the pan drippings.

Sauté the potatoes, onion, bell peppers, oregano and red pepper flakes in the reserved pan drippings for 10 to 15 minutes or until the vegetables are tender. Stir in the undrained tomatoes, broth and tomato paste. Bring to a boil and remove from the heat. Return the chicken to the skillet and bake, covered, at 350 degrees for 30 minutes. Serve immediately.

NUTRIENTS PER SERVING — **Yield: 4 servings**

CAL	PROT	CARBO	T FAT	SAT. FAT	MONOUFA	FIBER	SOD	OMEGA-3 FA	K
323	29G	36G	7G	2G	4G	5G	733MG	<1G	1061MG

PER SERVING	CARB CHOICES	2	CARB SOURCES				

61

Chicken Paprika

4	(6-ounce) boneless skinless chicken breasts	1/2	cup finely chopped onion
1 1/2	tablespoons sweet paprika	1 1/2	tablespoons sweet paprika
1/2	teaspoon salt	4	plum tomatoes, cut into 1/2-inch pieces
1/4	teaspoon freshly ground pepper	3/4	cup water
2	tablespoons butter	2/3	cup reduced-fat sour cream

Cut the chicken crosswise into 1/2-inch strips and toss with 1 1/2 tablespoons paprika, the salt and pepper in a bowl until coated. Heat 1 tablespoon of the butter in a large skillet over medium-high heat. Cook the chicken in the butter for 4 to 5 minutes or until cooked through. Remove the chicken to a platter using tongs, reserving the pan drippings.

Heat the remaining 1 tablespoon butter with the reserved pan drippings over medium heat. Add the onion to the butter mixture and cook for 5 to 6 minutes or until the onion is tender, stirring frequently to dislodge any brown bits from the bottom of the skillet. Stir in 1 1/2 tablespoons paprika and cook for 30 seconds, stirring constantly. Add the tomatoes and water and cook for 4 to 5 minutes or until of a sauce consistency, stirring occasionally. Return the chicken and any accumulated juices to the skillet. Stir in the sour cream and cook just until heated through; do not boil.

NUTRIENTS PER SERVING   Yield: 4 servings

CAL	PROT	CARBO	T FAT	SAT. FAT	MONOUFA	FIBER	SOD	OMEGA-3 FA	K
329	38G	10G	15G	8G	3G	3G	403MG	<1G	658MG

PER SERVING	CARB CHOICES	1/2	CARB SOURCES		OTHER SOURCES	

Kung Pao Chicken

3	tablespoons cornstarch
1/2	cup fat-free reduced-sodium chicken broth
3	tablespoons low-sodium soy sauce
2	tablespoons rice wine vinegar
1	tablespoon minced garlic
3/4	teaspoon hot red pepper sauce
2	teaspoons brown sugar
2	teaspoons sesame oil

1	pound boneless skinless chicken breasts, coarsely chopped
1	(8-ounce) can water chestnuts, drained, rinsed and chopped
1	red bell pepper, finely chopped
1/2	cup finely chopped carrots
1/4	cup chopped peanuts
2	cups brown rice, cooked

Combine the cornstarch and broth in a bowl and whisk until the cornstarch dissolves. Stir in the soy sauce, vinegar, garlic, hot sauce, brown sugar and 1 teaspoon of the sesame oil.

Coat a large nonstick skillet or wok with nonstick cooking spray and add the remaining 1 teaspoon sesame oil. Heat over medium-high heat and add the chicken. Stir-fry for 4 minutes. Remove the chicken to a bowl using a slotted spoon, reserving the pan drippings.

Add the water chestnuts, bell pepper, carrots and peanuts to the reserved pan drippings and stir-fry for 4 minutes. Stir in the broth mixture and bring to a boil. Return the chicken to the skillet and simmer for 3 minutes, stirring occasionally. Serve over the hot cooked brown rice.

Keep hot foods hot and cold foods cold. Bacteria double in number very quickly if foods are not kept at correct temperatures. To prevent food poisoning, avoid holding cold foods over 40 degrees and hot foods under 140 degrees. After serving, do not leave food at room temperature for more than two hours.

NUTRIENTS PER SERVING   Yield: 4 servings

CAL	PROT	CARBO	T FAT	SAT. FAT	MONOUFA	FIBER	SOD	OMEGA-3 FA	K
625	35G	94G	12G	2G	4G	8G	454MG	<1G	606MG

PER SERVING	CARB CHOICES	6	CARB SOURCES		AND OTHER SOURCES	

Meat, fish, and poultry contain heme iron, which is the form that is better absorbed than the non-heme iron in plant foods. When you eat plant foods along with even small amounts of meat, fish, or poultry, the non-heme iron in the plant foods is better absorbed.

Chicken Stir-Fry

1	cup low-sodium chicken broth	3/4	cup chopped fresh broccoli	
2	tablespoons low-sodium soy sauce	1/2	cup chopped carrots	
2	tablespoons Worcestershire sauce	1	(6-ounce) can sliced water chestnuts, drained	
1	cup chopped celery	1	(6-ounce) can sliced mushrooms, drained	
1/2	cup chopped onion			
1/4	teaspoon garlic powder	1	(6-ounce) package frozen snow peas	
2	cups (1-inch) pieces boneless skinless chicken breasts			

Heat a wok and add the broth, soy sauce, Worcestershire sauce, celery, onion and garlic powder. Stir-fry for 1 minute. Add the chicken and stir-fry for 2 minutes. Add the broccoli, carrots, water chestnuts, mushrooms and snow peas and stir-fry until the vegetables are tender-crisp and the mixture is heated through. Serve over hot cooked rice or noodles.

NUTRIENTS PER SERVING   Yield: 4 (1-cup) servings

CAL	PROT	CARBO	T FAT	SAT. FAT	MONOUFA	FIBER	SOD	OMEGA-3 FA	K
209	27G	18G	3G	1G	1G	6G	575MG	<1G	657MG

PER SERVING	CARB CHOICES	1	CARB SOURCES		OTHER SOURCES	

Chicken with Asparagus
and New Potatoes

12	ounces fresh asparagus spears	**1**	tablespoon olive oil
1	pound small new potatoes, cut into quarters	**2**	teaspoons snipped fresh thyme
2	cups (10 ounces) shredded or chopped deli-roasted chicken	**1**	teaspoon finely shredded lemon zest

Snap off the thick woody ends of the asparagus spears and discard. Cut the spears into 2-inch pieces. Combine the potatoes with a small amount of boiling water in a medium saucepan. Cook, covered, for 12 minutes. Add the asparagus to the saucepan and cook, covered, for 2 to 4 minutes longer or until the potatoes are tender and the asparagus is tender-crisp.

Drain the vegetables and return to the saucepan. Stir in the chicken. Whisk the olive oil, thyme and lemon zest in a bowl and drizzle over the chicken mixture. Toss lightly to coat. Cook until a meat thermometer registers 160 degrees. Serve at 140 degrees.

NUTRIENTS PER SERVING   **Yield: 4 servings**

CAL	PROT	CARBO	T FAT	SAT. FAT	MONOUFA	FIBER	SOD	OMEGA-3 FA	K
254	22G	24G	8G	2G	4G	4G	61MG	<1G	949MG

PER SERVING	CARB CHOICES	**1 1/2**	CARB SOURCES				

Curried Turkey with Mint Riata Sauce

Marinade and Turkey

1/4	cup apple juice
1/3	cup canola oil
1	teaspoon cumin
1	teaspoon curry powder
1/2	teaspoon coriander
1/2	teaspoon mace
1/2	teaspoon turmeric
4	(3-ounce) portions turkey breast

Mint Riata Sauce

1	cup yogurt
1/2	cup honey
2	tablespoons chopped fresh mint
	Coarse salt and pepper to taste

For the marinade, mix the apple juice, canola oil, cumin, curry powder, coriander, mace and turmeric in a shallow dish. Add the turkey to the marinade and turn to coat. Marinate, covered, in the refrigerator for 8 to 10 hours, turning occasionally; drain. Grill the turkey over hot coals until a meat thermometer registers 170 degrees.

For the sauce, process the yogurt, honey, mint, salt and pepper in a blender until smooth. Drizzle over the turkey just before serving.

Nutritional profile includes 1 tablespoon of the marinade and 2 tablespoons of the sauce per serving.

NUTRIENTS PER SERVING   Yield: 4 servings

CAL	PROT	CARBO	T FAT	SAT. FAT	MONOUFA	FIBER	SOD	OMEGA-3 FA	K
223	21G	13G	9G	1G	5G	‹1G	45MG	1G	244MG

PER SERVING	CARB CHOICES	1	CARB SOURCES				

Grilled Fish Skewers

1	pound swordfish, skinned	1	garlic clove
1	pound salmon, skinned	1/8	teaspoon salt
24	cherry tomatoes	1/8	teaspoon freshly ground pepper
1	cup lightly packed fresh basil		Salt and pepper to taste
1/2	cup olive oil		

Cut the swordfish into twelve 11/2-inch cubes and cut the salmon into twelve 11/2-inch cubes. Thread the fish against the grain on 8 skewers alternating each cube with 1 cherry tomato.

Process the basil, olive oil and garlic in a blender until smooth Season with 1/8 teaspoon salt and 1/8 teaspoon pepper. Reserve 1/2 of the basil oil. Brush the remaining basil oil over the kabobs and sprinkle with salt and pepper to taste. Grill over medium heat for 6 to 10 minutes or until the fish is opaque, turning occasionally. Coat the kabobs with the reserved basil oil using a clean brush and serve immediately.

To boost brain health, current research supports what we already know for the prevention of chronic diseases—less saturated and trans fats; more unsaturated fats, such as in nuts, seeds, fish, olive oil, and canola oil; and more fruits and vegetables.

NUTRIENTS PER SERVING — **Yield: 4 (2-kabob) servings**

CAL	PROT	CARBO	T FAT	SAT. FAT	MONOUFA	FIBER	SOD	OMEGA-3 FA	K
596	48G	6G	42G	7G	27G	2G	241MG	2G	949MG

PER SERVING	CARB CHOICES	0	CARB SOURCES				

Orange Roughy with Kiwifruit and Walnuts

1 tablespoon vegetable oil	1/3 cup chicken broth
2 (4-ounce) orange roughy fillets	1/3 cup orange juice
1 tablespoon trans-fat-free margarine or butter	11/2 teaspoons chopped fresh basil, or 1/2 teaspoon dried basil
2 tablespoons coarsely chopped walnuts	1 kiwifruit, cut lengthwise into halves and sliced
11/2 teaspoons cornstarch	2 cups hot cooked rice
1/4 teaspoon salt	

Heat the oil in a 10-inch skillet over medium heat. Cook the fillets in the hot oil for 8 minutes or until the fillets flake easily with a fork, carefully turning once. Remove the fillets from the skillet to a platter and cover to keep warm. Drain the pan drippings from the skillet.

Melt the margarine in the same skillet over medium heat. Stir in the walnuts and cook until golden brown, stirring frequently. Remove the walnuts with a slotted spoon to a plate, reserving the pan drippings.

Stir the cornstarch and salt into the reserved pan drippings until blended. Add the broth, orange juice and basil and bring to a boil, stirring constantly. Boil for 1 minute, stirring constantly. Add the kiwifruit and stir gently until coated. Spoon the sauce over the fillets and sprinkle with the walnuts. Serve over the rice.

NUTRIENTS PER SERVING   Yield: 2 servings

CAL	PROT	CARBO	T FAT	SAT. FAT	MONOUFA	FIBER	SOD	OMEGA-3 FA	K
498	24G	57G	19G	2G	6G	3G	509MG	1G	677MG

PER SERVING	CARB CHOICES	4	CARB SOURCES				

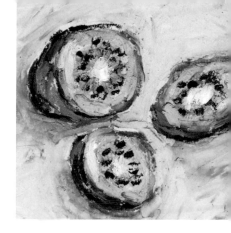

Garlic Lime Salmon

1/2 cup extra-virgin olive oil	1 garlic clove, minced
1 small onion, chopped	2 (1 1/2-pound) salmon fillets
2 tablespoons lime juice	Lime slices
1 teaspoon grated lime zest	

Whisk the olive oil, onion, lime juice, lime zest and garlic in a bowl. Arrange the fillets on a broiler rack in a broiler pan. Broil 4 to 6 inches from the heat source for 20 minutes or until the fillets flake easily, basting every 5 minutes with the lime mixture. Garnish with lime slices.

What are the food sources of Omega-3 fats? Cold-water fatty fish such as salmon, herring, albacore tuna, mackerel, and sardines are good sources. Eating fish two to three times per week is encouraged. Plant sources of Omega-3 are flaxseed meal, flaxseed oil, canola oil, walnuts, and avocados.

NUTRIENTS PER SERVING — Yield: 6 servings

CAL	PROT	CARBO	T FAT	SAT. FAT	MONOUFA	FIBER	SOD	OMEGA-3 FA	K
582	52G	2G	39G	6G	24G	<1G	125MG	3G	731MG

PER SERVING	CARB CHOICES	0	CARB SOURCES				

Poached Salmon with Cucumber Dill Sauce

Cucumber Dill Sauce

3/4	cup lite sour cream
1/3	cup chopped peeled cucumber
2	tablespoons snipped fresh dill weed
1	tablespoon fresh lemon juice
1/8	teaspoon freshly ground pepper

Salmon

1 1/2	cups water
1	cup reduced-sodium chicken broth
2	scallions, sliced
8	black peppercorns
4	(4-ounce) salmon fillets
	Sprigs of dill weed

For the sauce, combine the sour cream, cucumber, dill weed, lemon juice and pepper in a bowl and mix well. Chill, covered, until serving time.

For the salmon, pour the water into a large nonstick skillet. Stir in the broth, scallions and peppercorns. Arrange the salmon in a single layer in the broth mixture and bring just to a boil over high heat. Reduce the heat to medium-low and simmer, covered, for 6 minutes or until the fillets flake easily with a fork. Remove the fillets to a serving platter and garnish with sprigs of dill weed. Serve hot or chilled with the sauce.

NUTRIENTS PER SERVING **Yield: 4 servings**

CAL	PROT	CARBO	T FAT	SAT. FAT	MONOUFA	FIBER	SOD	OMEGA-3 FA	K
273	30G	4G	14G	5G	5G	‹1G	233MG	1G	559MG

PER SERVING	CARB CHOICES	0	CARB SOURCES				

Tarragon Pecan Salmon

4 (6-ounce) salmon fillets

1/4 cup orange juice

2 tablespoons olive oil

2 teaspoons grated orange zest

2 teaspoons snipped fresh tarragon

1 tablespoon Dijon mustard

1 tablespoon butter, melted

1 teaspoon honey

1/4 cup fine dry multigrain bread crumbs

1/4 cup finely chopped pecans

2 teaspoons snipped fresh tarragon

1 teaspoon snipped fresh parsley

Snipped fresh tarragon (optional)

Snipped fresh parsley (optional)

Lemon slices (optional)

Rinse the fillets and pat dry with paper towels. Place the fillets in a large sealable plastic bag and set in a deep bowl. Combine the orange juice, olive oil, orange zest and 2 teaspoons tarragon in a bowl and mix well. Pour the orange juice mixture over the fillets and seal the bag. Turn to coat and let stand at room temperature for 20 minutes, turning occasionally.

Mix the Dijon mustard, butter, and honey in a bowl. Toss the bread crumbs, pecans, 2 teaspoons tarragon and parsley in a small bowl. Remove the fillets from the marinade and discard the marinade.

Arrange the fillets skin side down in a greased shallow baking pan. Brush the fillets with the mustard mixture and sprinkle with the bread crumb mixture, pressing gently to coat. Bake at 425 degrees for 12 to 16 minutes or until the fillets flake easily with a fork. Sprinkle with additional tarragon and parsley and garnish with lemon slices.

Zest: The colorful rind of citrus fruit (most commonly lemon, lime, or orange), contains aromatic oils that add flavor to food. Be careful not to include any of the white pith, which adds a bitter taste.

Nutritional profile includes the entire amount of the marinade.

NUTRIENTS PER SERVING — Yield: 4 servings

CAL	PROT	CARBO	T FAT	SAT. FAT	MONOUFA	FIBER	SOD	OMEGA-3 FA	K
478	40G	8G	31G	6G	16G	1G	212MG	2G	602MG

PER SERVING	CARB CHOICES	1/2	CARB SOURCES				

Seared Tuna with Clementine Salsa

Clementine Salsa

1   **cup clementine sections (about 6 to 8 clementines)**

1/4   **cup minced red onion**

2   **tablespoons fresh lime juice**

2   **tablespoons chopped fresh cilantro**

    Salt and pepper to taste

Tuna and Assembly

6   **cups water**

2   **cups brown rice**

1   **teaspoon oregano**

1   **zucchini, finely chopped**

1/8   **teaspoon coarse salt**

    Freshly ground pepper to taste

4   **(4-ounce) tuna steaks**

2   **teaspoons Caribbean jerk seasoning (such as McCormick)**

2   **teaspoons extra-virgin olive oil**

For the salsa, combine the clementine sections, onion, lime juice and cilantro in a bowl and mix well. Season to taste with salt and pepper. You may substitute orange sections or tangerine sections for the clementine sections.

For the tuna, bring the water to a boil in a medium saucepan over high heat. Stir in the brown rice and oregano and reduce the heat to low. Simmer, covered, until the rice is tender. Remove from the heat and stir in the zucchini. Let stand, covered, for 6 minutes or until the zucchini is tender. Fluff with a fork and season with the salt and pepper. Sprinkle both sides of the steaks with the jerk seasoning. Heat the olive oil in a large nonstick skillet over medium-high heat. Cook the steaks in the hot oil for 2 minutes per side for medium-rare or 3 to 4 minutes per side for well done. Remove the steaks to a platter and cover to keep warm.

To serve, arrange 1 steak on each of 4 serving plates. Top each steak with 1/4 of the salsa and spoon 1/4 of the rice mixture next to each steak. Serve immediately.

NUTRIENTS PER SERVING   Yield: 4 servings

CAL	PROT	CARBO	T FAT	SAT. FAT	MONOUFA	FIBER	SOD	OMEGA-3 FA	K
565	36G	80G	11G	2G	5G	5G	257MG	1G	735MG

PER SERVING	CARB CHOICES	5	CARB SOURCES				

Garlic-Marinated
Seafood Brochettes

Garlic Purée

1   **head garlic, cloves separated and peeled**

1/16 **teaspoon salt**

Seafood Brochettes

1¹/2 **cups low-fat plain yogurt**

1/3 **cup chopped fresh cilantro**

1/2 **teaspoon salt**

1/8 **teaspoon ground red pepper (optional)**

1   **(1-pound) salmon steak, cut into 12 cubes**

12 **large scallops**

12 **jumbo shrimp, peeled and deveined**

For the purée, simmer the garlic in enough water to cover in a saucepan for 10 minutes. Drain, reserving 2 tablespoons of the cooking liquid. Combine the garlic, reserved cooking liquid and salt in a food processor and process until puréed. Store, covered, in the refrigerator.

For the brochettes, whisk 1/4 cup purée, the yogurt, cilantro, salt and red pepper in a bowl. Reserve 1/2 cup of the yogurt mixture. Alternately thread 3 salmon cubes, 3 scallops and 3 shrimp on each of 4 metal or wooden skewers. Skewer the shrimp twice, so the skewer passes through the shrimp close to both of the ends. If using wooden skewers soak in water for 20 minutes prior to threading. Arrange the brochettes in a shallow dish and pour the remaining yogurt mixture over the brochettes, turning to coat. Broil or grill over hot coals for 15 to 20 minutes or until the salmon flakes easily, the scallops are tender and the shrimp turn pink, brushing with the reserved yogurt mixture halfway through the broiling or grilling process.

Never baste fish, poultry, or meat with a marinade that was used to marinate uncooked food. Double the marinade recipe instead, reserving half for grilling.

Nutritional profile includes 1 tablespoon of the garlic purée per serving.

NUTRIENTS PER BROCHETTE   **Yield: 4 brochettes**

CAL	PROT	CARBO	T FAT	SAT. FAT	MONOUFA	FIBER	SOD	OMEGA-3 FA	K
345	46G	8G	12G	3G	5G	<1G	603MG	1G	760MG

PER SERVING	CARB CHOICES	1/2	CARB SOURCES				

Watch out for trans fat, a fatty acid produced when liquid oil is hydrogenated to form a solid fat, such as shortening or stick margarine. Use tub or liquid margarines that are labeled "0 Trans" and limit high-fat snack foods. Use olive oil, canola oil, or nonstick cooking spray for cooking and baking instead of stick margarine, butter, or shortening.

entreés

Shrimp and Tomatoes

6	plum tomatoes
1	tablespoon plus 2 teaspoons olive oil
1 1/2	pounds shrimp, peeled and deveined
1/8	teaspoon coarse salt
	Freshly ground black pepper to taste

3	garlic cloves, thinly sliced
1/8	teaspoon red pepper flakes
	Salt to taste
2	tablespoons chopped fresh parsley
2	tablespoons fresh lemon juice

Cut the tomatoes lengthwise into halves and cut each half into 1/2-inch slices. Heat 1 tablespoon of the olive oil in a large nonstick skillet over high heat and swirl to coat the bottom of the pan. Season the shrimp with 1/8 teaspoon salt and black pepper. Add 1/2 of the shrimp to the hot oil and cook for 3 to 4 minutes or until the shrimp are opaque, stirring and turning frequently. Remove the shrimp to a platter using a slotted spoon, reserving the pan drippings.

Heat the remaining 2 teaspoons olive oil with the reserved pan drippings and repeat the process with the remaining shrimp. Remove the shrimp using a slotted spoon to the platter, reserving the pan drippings. Reduce the heat to medium and stir the garlic and red pepper flakes into the reserved pan drippings. Add the tomatoes and cook for 4 to 6 minutes or until the tomatoes begin to break down, stirring occasionally. Season to taste with salt.

Return the shrimp and any accumulated juices to the skillet and mix gently. Stir in the parsley and lemon juice. Serve over hot cooked pasta, rice or steamed spinach, if desired.

NUTRIENTS PER SERVING   Yield: 4 servings

CAL	PROT	CARBO	T FAT	SAT. FAT	MONOUFA	FIBER	SOD	OMEGA-3 FA	K
200	28G	5G	7G	1G	4G	1G	356MG	<1G	485MG

PER SERVING	CARB CHOICES	0	CARB SOURCES				

Zesty Shrimp Scampi

2	tablespoons olive oil
1	pound large shrimp, peeled and deveined
3	garlic cloves, minced
1/2	cup dry white wine

1	teaspoon freshly grated lemon zest
1/4	teaspoon coarse salt
1/4	teaspoon freshly ground pepper
1/2	cup chopped fresh parsley

Heat the olive oil in a large skillet and add the shrimp. Cook for 2 minutes, stirring frequently. Stir in the garlic and cook for 1 minute. Add the wine, lemon zest, salt and pepper and bring to a boil.

Cook for 2 minutes, stirring occasionally. Add the parsley and toss until the shrimp are coated and opaque. Serve with hot cooked pasta or rice or on a bed of greens.

NUTRIENTS PER SERVING — **Yield: 4 servings**

CAL	PROT	CARBO	T FAT	SAT. FAT	MONOUFA	FIBER	SOD	OMEGA-3 FA	K
171	18G	2G	8G	1G	5G	<1G	319MG	<1G	232MG

PER SERVING	CARB CHOICES	0	CARB SOURCES					

Carotenoids are powerful antioxidants that help protect the body from damaging compounds. They have also been shown to promote healthy vision. Carotenoids like alpha-carotene, beta-carotene, lutein, and lycopene are found in red, yellow, and orange fruits, and dark green leafy vegetables.

Beef and Spinach Lasagna

Basic White Sauce

- 1 **cup skim milk**
- 1 **tablespoon cornstarch**
- 1/2 **teaspoon salt (optional)**
- 1/4 **teaspoon white pepper (optional)**

Lasagna

- 1/2 **cup (2 ounces) freshly grated Parmesan cheese**
- 1 **pound lean ground beef**
- 1 **(10-ounce) package frozen chopped spinach, thawed and drained**
- 3 **cups spaghetti sauce**
- 9 **whole wheat lasagna noodles, cooked and drained**
- 8 **ounces low-fat mozzarella cheese, shredded**

For the sauce, whisk the skim milk and cornstarch in a saucepan until blended. Bring to a boil over medium-high heat and reduce the heat, stirring constantly. Cook for 3 to 5 minutes or until thickened, stirring constantly. Season with the salt and white pepper.

For the lasagna, stir all but 1 to 2 tablespoons of the Parmesan cheese into the white sauce in a bowl and set aside. Brown the ground beef in a nonstick skillet, stirring until crumbly; drain. Press the excess moisture from the spinach.

Spread about 3/4 cup of the spaghetti sauce over the bottom of a greased 9×13-inch baking pan. Layer with 3 noodles, 1/2 of the spinach, 1/2 of the ground beef, 1/3 of the white sauce mixture and 3/4 cup of the remaining spaghetti sauce. Repeat this layering process, ending with the remaining 3 noodles, the remaining white sauce mixture, the mozzarella cheese, the remaining spaghetti sauce and the remaining Parmesan cheese.

Bake, covered with foil, at 350 degrees for 30 to 35 minutes. Remove the foil and bake for 10 to 15 minutes longer or until light brown. Let stand for 5 minutes before serving.

NUTRIENTS PER SERVING   **Yield: 9 (3×4-inch) servings**

CAL	PROT	CARBO	T FAT	SAT. FAT	MONOUFA	FIBER	SOD	OMEGA-3 FA	K
426	28G	40G	17G	7G	6G	8G	552MG	<1G	626MG

| PER SERVING | CARB CHOICES | 2 1/2 | CARB SOURCES | | | | |

Asian-Style Pasta Primavera

3	large shiitake mushrooms (3 inches in diameter), or 2 ounces large fresh white mushrooms
3/4	cup low-sodium chicken broth
1	tablespoon low-sodium soy sauce
1/2	teaspoon sugar
1/2	teaspoon wine vinegar
2	tablespoons sesame seeds
3	quarts water
8	ounces angel hair pasta
2	tablespoons olive oil
2	ounces thinly sliced cooked ham, cut into julienne strips
2	garlic cloves, minced or crushed
1	tablespoon minced fresh ginger
1	small head baby bok choy, trimmed and thinly sliced
4	ounces Chinese pea pods (snow peas), trimmed and strings removed
2	tablespoons dry sherry

If using shiitake mushrooms, trim and discard the tough stems and thinly slice the shiitake or white mushrooms. Mix the broth, soy sauce, sugar and vinegar in a bowl. Toast the sesame seeds in a skillet or wok over medium heat for 6 to 8 minutes or until golden brown, shaking the skillet frequently. Remove the sesame seeds to a plate to cool.

Bring the water to a boil in a 5- or 6-quart saucepan and add the pasta. Cook for 5 minutes or until al dente. Drain and cover to keep warm. Heat the skillet used to toast the sesame seeds over high heat. Add the olive oil and ham and cook for 2 minutes or until the ham is light brown, stirring constantly. Remove the ham using a slotted spoon to a plate, reserving the pan drippings. Add the garlic and ginger to the reserved pan drippings and cook for 30 seconds or until fragrant, stirring constantly. Stir in the mushrooms, bok choy, pea pods and sherry.

Cook for 2 minutes or until the pea pods turn bright green and are tender-crisp, stirring constantly. Add the broth mixture and bring to a boil. Remove from the heat. Add the pasta and ham to the pea pod mixture and toss lightly using 2 forks. Spoon equal portions of the pasta mixture onto 2 serving plates and sprinkle with the sesame seeds.

NUTRIENTS PER SERVING   **Yield: 4 servings**

CAL	PROT	CARBO	T FAT	SAT. FAT	MONOUFA	FIBER	SOD	OMEGA-3 FA	K
358	16G	50G	11G	2G	6G	5G	184MG	<1G	517MG

PER SERVING	CARB CHOICES	3	CARB SOURCES				

Chicken Linguini

2	tablespoons olive oil		2	tablespoons chopped fresh basil
4	ounces boneless skinless chicken breasts, cut into 1/4×11/2-inch strips		1	tablespoon finely chopped shallot
1/2	cup sliced fresh shiitake mushrooms		2	teaspoons minced garlic
				Freshly ground pepper to taste
1/2	cup low-fat chicken stock		1	tablespoon butter
1/2	cup chopped seeded fresh tomato		4	ounces spinach linguini, cooked and drained
1/4	cup chopped roasted tomato		1/4	cup (1 ounce) freshly grated Parmesan cheese

Heat the olive oil in a medium skillet over high heat until hot but not smoking. Sauté the chicken and mushrooms in the hot oil for 1 minute. Stir in the stock, fresh tomato, roasted tomato, basil, shallot and garlic.

Cook over high heat until the liquid is reduced by 3/4, stirring occasionally. Season to taste with pepper. Add the butter and pasta and toss to mix. Cook just until heated through, stirring frequently. Spoon onto a heated serving platter and sprinkle with the cheese.

NUTRIENTS PER SERVING   Yield: 2 servings

CAL	PROT	CARBO	T FAT	SAT. FAT	MONOUFA	FIBER	SOD	OMEGA-3 FA	K
387	21G	21G	24G	8G	13G	2G	290MG	‹1G	319MG

PER SERVING	CARB CHOICES	11/2	CARB SOURCES		OTHER SOURCES	

Linguini with Scallops

1 pound sea scallops, bay scallops or calico scallops

1/4 cup olive oil

2 garlic cloves, minced

1/8 teaspoon salt

1/8 teaspoon freshly ground pepper

1/4 cup plain bread crumbs, toasted

1/2 cup minced fresh parsley

16 ounces linguini or spaghetti

Salt to taste

1 tablespoon olive oil

Bring a large saucepan of water to a boil. Cut the sea scallops into 1/4- to 1/2-inch pieces, cut the bay scallops into halves and leave the calico scallops whole. Combine 1/4 cup olive oil and the garlic in a small saucepan and cook over low heat until the garlic turns pale tan, stirring occasionally. Increase the heat to medium-high and stir in the scallops, 1/8 teaspoon salt and the pepper.

Cook for 2 minutes or just until the surface of the scallops turn opaque, stirring frequently. Stir in the bread crumbs and 1/4 cup of the parsley. Remove from the heat and cover to keep warm. Add the pasta and salt to taste to the boiling water and boil until al dente. Reheat the scallop mixture just before the pasta is done.

Drain the pasta, reserving the cooking liquid. Toss the pasta, scallop mixture, 1 tablespoon olive oil and a small amount of the reserved cooking liquid if necessary in a pasta bowl and sprinkle with the remaining 1/4 cup parsley. Serve immediately.

NUTRIENTS PER SERVING
Yield: 4 servings

CAL	PROT	CARBO	T FAT	SAT. FAT	MONOUFA	FIBER	SOD	OMEGA-3 FA	K
723	40G	92G	20G	3G	13G	4G	413MG	<1G	527MG

PER SERVING	CARB CHOICES	6	CARB SOURCES				

Shrimp and Angel Hair Pasta

Peeling shrimp is a bit tedious, so if you can buy your shrimp already peeled, go for it. Or, peel shrimp the night before or in the morning to speed up meal preparation.

2	teaspoons olive oil		1/2	teaspoon oregano
2	garlic cloves, minced		1	pound large shrimp, peeled and deveined
2	(14-ounce) cans reduced-sodium stewed tomatoes		2	ounces feta cheese, crumbled
1/4	cup white wine		8	ounces angel hair pasta, cooked and drained
2	tablespoons lemon juice		1/4	teaspoon minced fresh parsley

Heat the olive oil in a large nonstick skillet. Cook the garlic in the hot oil for 2 to 3 minutes or until tender. Stir in the undrained tomatoes, wine, lemon juice and oregano. Add the shrimp and toss to mix.

Simmer, covered, for 4 to 5 minutes or until the shrimp turn pink, stirring occasionally. Remove from the heat and stir in the cheese. Spoon the shrimp sauce over the hot cooked pasta on a serving platter and sprinkle with the parsley.

NUTRIENTS PER SERVING   **Yield: 4 servings**

CAL	PROT	CARBO	T FAT	SAT. FAT	MONOUFA	FIBER	SOD	OMEGA-3 FA	K
417	29G	58G	8G	3G	3G	5G	437MG	‹1G	299MG

PER SERVING	CARB CHOICES	4	CARB SOURCES				

Garden Vegetables with Penne Pasta

2 tablespoons extra-virgin olive oil	**1/3** cup chopped fresh basil
3/4 cup chopped onion	**1/3** cup low-sodium chicken broth
1/2 cup (1 1/2-inch) slices red bell pepper	**1** tablespoon tomato paste
1 1/2 tablespoons minced fresh garlic	**1** tablespoon balsamic vinegar
1 1/2 cups (1/4-inch) slices zucchini, cut into halves	**1/2** teaspoon cayenne pepper
1 1/2 cups (1/4-inch) slices yellow squash, cut into halves	**1/4** teaspoon dried oregano
	1/4 teaspoon dried thyme
8 ounces cooked shrimp or chicken (optional)	**1/4** teaspoon black pepper
1 1/2 cups chopped fresh tomatoes	**1/3** pound whole wheat penne pasta, cooked and drained
	1/4 cup (1 ounce) freshly grated Parmesan cheese

Heat a 12- or 16-inch skillet over high heat. Add the olive oil and onion to the hot skillet and sauté for 3 minutes. Add the bell pepper and garlic and sauté for 3 minutes. Add the zucchini and yellow squash and sauté for 3 minutes. Stir in the shrimp, tomatoes, basil, broth, tomato paste, vinegar, cayenne pepper, oregano, thyme and black pepper and sauté for 5 minutes longer.

Toss the squash mixture with the pasta in a pasta bowl until combined. Serve with the cheese.

Teach your taste buds to enjoy herbs and spices in place of salt. Basil, dill weed, marjoram, parsley, rosemary, sage, savory, tarragon, and thyme are just some of the herbs that can replace salt in your cooking.

NUTRIENTS PER SERVING | Yield: 2 servings

CAL	PROT	CARBO	T FAT	SAT. FAT	MONOUFA	FIBER	SOD	OMEGA-3 FA	K
556	22G	80G	19G	4G	12G	6G	266MG	<1G	1128MG

PER SERVING	CARB CHOICES	**5**	CARB SOURCES				

Does the recipe call
for an onion but there
isn't one in your
vegetable bin? Use
1 teaspoon onion
powder or 1 tablespoon
minced dried onion.

entreés

Pine Nut Penne Pasta

1/4 cup pine nuts	2 tablespoon extra-virgin olive oil
16 ounces spinach penne pasta	1 cup part-skim ricotta cheese
1 1/2 pounds baby spinach, trimmed	1/4 cup (1 ounce) grated Parmesan cheese
1/4 cup chopped onion	
1 garlic clove, minced	

Spread the pine nuts in a single layer on a baking sheet with sides and toast at 350 degrees for 6 to 8 minutes or until golden brown, stirring occasionally. Cook the penne using the package directions, adding the spinach during the last 2 minutes of the cooking process. Drain and place the pasta mixture in a serving bowl.

Sauté the onion and garlic in 1 tablespoon of the olive oil in a skillet until the onion is tender. Add the onion mixture and remaining 1 tablespoon olive oil to the pasta mixture and toss to mix. Stir in the ricotta cheese, Parmesan cheese and pine nuts and serve immediately.

NUTRIENTS PER SERVING   **Yield: 6 servings**

CAL	PROT	CARBO	T FAT	SAT. FAT	MONOUFA	FIBER	SOD	OMEGA-3 FA	K
442	20G	61G	15G	4G	6G	6G	218MG	‹1G	1018MG

PER SERVING	CARB CHOICES	4	CARB SOURCES				

Roasted Zucchini and Tomato Pasta

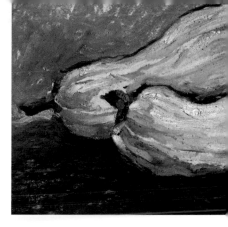

2   pounds zucchini, trimmed and cut into 1/2-inch slices

1   pound plum tomatoes, cut into 3/4-inch chunks

3   garlic cloves, thinly sliced

5   tablespoons olive oil

1/8   teaspoon salt

Freshly ground pepper to taste

1   pound long fusilli pasta or whole wheat linguini

Salt to taste

1   tablespoon olive oil

2   tablespoons chopped fresh parsley

1/4   cup (1 ounce) grated Parmesan cheese

Toss the zucchini, tomatoes and garlic with 5 tablespoons olive oil on a baking sheet with sides until coated. Sprinkle with 1/8 teaspoon salt and pepper. Spread the zucchini mixture in a single layer on the baking sheet and roast at 450 degrees for 20 to 25 minutes or until light brown, stirring occasionally. Remove the vegetable mixture to a bowl, reserving the baking sheet.

Cook the pasta in boiling salted water in a large saucepan for 12 minutes or until al dente. Drain, reserving 1/2 cup of the cooking liquid. Return the pasta to the saucepan and add 1 tablespoon olive oil, tossing to coat; cover. Pour the reserved cooking liquid onto the baking sheet used to roast the vegetables and scrape with a wooden spoon to dislodge any brown bits. Add the cooking liquid and roasted vegetables to the pasta and toss to mix. Add the parsley and cheese and mix well. Serve with additional Parmesan cheese, if desired.

NUTRIENTS PER SERVING   Yield: 6 servings

CAL	PROT	CARBO	T FAT	SAT. FAT	MONOUFA	FIBER	SOD	OMEGA-3 FA	K
444	12G	65G	16G	2G	10G	4G	120MG	<1G	593MG

PER SERVING	CARB CHOICES	4	CARB SOURCES				

Eggplant Parmesan

1/4	cup canola oil		1	Omega-3-enhanced egg
1/4	cup finely chopped onion		1/4	cup skim milk
1	garlic clove, crushed		1	tablespoon canola oil
3	(8-ounce) cans reduced-sodium tomato sauce			Flour to taste
1	tablespoon minced fresh parsley		2	tablespoons canola oil
1/4	teaspoon pepper		8	ounces mozzarella cheese, sliced
1	eggplant		1/2	cup (2 ounces) grated Parmesan cheese
	Juice of 1 lemon			

Heat 1/4 cup canola oil in a large skillet and add the onion and garlic. Cook over low heat until the onion is tender and yellow, stirring occasionally. Stir in the tomato sauce, parsley and pepper. Simmer for 30 minutes or until of a sauce consistency, stirring occasionally.

Peel the eggplant and cut into 1/4-inch slices. Brush each slice with the lemon juice to prevent discoloration. Whisk the egg lightly in a bowl. Add the skim milk and 1 tablespoon canola oil and whisk until blended. Dust each slice of the eggplant lightly with flour and tap to remove any excess. Dip the eggplant slices in the egg mixture and drain.

Heat 2 tablespoons canola oil in a large skillet over medium heat. Fry the eggplant on both sides in the hot oil until golden brown, adding additional canola oil if needed; drain. Layer the sauce, eggplant and mozzarella cheese in a 2-quart baking dish and sprinkle with the Parmesan cheese. Bake at 350 degrees for 30 minutes.

NUTRIENTS PER SERVING — **Yield: 6 servings**

CAL	PROT	CARBO	T FAT	SAT. FAT	MONOUFA	FIBER	SOD	OMEGA-3 FA	K
363	13G	15G	28G	7G	13G	4G	394MG	2G	264MG

PER SERVING	CARB CHOICES	1	CARB SOURCES				

Roasted Vegetable Wraps
with Chive Sauce

2   (8-ounce) zucchini

1   tablespoon olive oil

1   tablespoon rice vinegar

1   teaspoon chopped fresh rosemary

1   garlic clove, minced

1/4   teaspoon salt

2   large red bell peppers, each cut into 8 strips

1   large red onion, cut into 16 wedges

8   (7-inch) whole wheat tortillas

3/4   cup low-fat plain yogurt, drained

1   tablespoon snipped fresh chives

1/8   teaspoon onion powder

Place the oven rack in the upper third of the oven. Cut the zucchini crosswise into halves, then lengthwise into 1/4-inch slices. Whisk the olive oil, vinegar, rosemary, garlic and salt in a bowl until combined.

Toss the zucchini, bell peppers and onion with the olive oil mixture on a 10x15-inch baking sheet sprayed lightly with nonstick cooking spray. Roast at 450 degrees for 30 minutes or until brown, tossing frequently. Mist the tortillas with water and wrap in foil. Place the tortillas in the oven 5 minutes before the end of the roasting process.

Mix the yogurt, chives and onion powder in a small bowl. Spread the yogurt mixture evenly on 1 side of each warm tortilla and top with equal portions of the roasted vegetables. Fold in the sides of the tortillas and roll tightly to enclose the filling. Cut each wrap diagonally into 3 pieces.

If a recipe calls for fresh herbs and you do not have any available, substitute one teaspoon of crushed dried herbs for each tablespoon of fresh herbs.

NUTRIENTS PER SERVING   Yield: 8 (3-piece) servings

CAL	PROT	CARBO	T FAT	SAT. FAT	MONOUFA	FIBER	SOD	OMEGA-3 FA	K
134	6G	28G	3G	1G	1G	4G	263MG	<1G	512MG

PER SERVING	CARB CHOICES	2	CARB SOURCES				

Zucchini and Tomato Frittata

2	tablespoons olive oil
3	zucchini, cut into 1/4-inch slices (11/2 pounds)
1/2	cup finely chopped onion
1	tablespoon fresh thyme leaves
1/2	teaspoon salt
	Freshly ground black pepper to taste
8	Omega-3-enhanced eggs
3/4	cup (3 ounces) shredded white Cheddar cheese or sharp Cheddar cheese
1/4	cup milk
1/4	teaspoon red pepper flakes
	Salt to taste
3	vine-ripened tomatoes, thinly sliced crosswise (1 pound)

Heat the olive oil in a 10-inch nonstick ovenproof skillet. Add the zucchini, onion and thyme to the hot oil and cook, covered, for 7 to 8 minutes or until the vegetables are tender and light brown, stirring frequently. Remove the cover and cook until the liquid evaporates, stirring occasionally. Stir in the salt and generously season with black pepper. Remove from the heat.

Whisk the eggs, cheese, milk and red pepper flakes in a bowl until combined. Season to taste with salt and pepper. Pour the egg mixture over the vegetables, gently lifting the vegetables to allow the egg mixture to coat the bottom of the skillet. Arrange the sliced tomatoes over the top.

Bake at 425 degrees for 10 to 15 minutes or until the center is firm and the tomatoes are brown. Gently loosen the side of the frittata with a spatula and cut into 8 wedges.

NUTRIENTS PER SERVING　　　　　　　　　　　　　　　　**Yield: 8 servings**

CAL	PROT	CARBO	T FAT	SAT. FAT	MONOUFA	FIBER	SOD	OMEGA-3 FA	K
178	12G	7G	11G	3G	5G	2G	288MG	‹1G	628MG

PER SERVING	CARB CHOICES	1/2	CARB SOURCES				

Walnut Waffles

1/2	cup ground flaxseed	1/4	teaspoon coarse salt
1/2	cup chopped walnuts	4	Omega-3-enhanced eggs
1/2	cup ground almonds	1	cup 1% milk
1/4	cup sugar	1	teaspoon baking powder
2	teaspoons ground cinnamon		

Combine the flaxseed, walnuts, almonds, sugar, cinnamon and salt in a blender or food processor and process until the walnuts are ground. Whisk the eggs and 1/2 cup of the milk in a bowl until blended. Add the flaxseed mixture and mix well.

Chill, covered, for 1 to 10 hours. Whisk in the remaining 1/2 cup milk and the baking powder just before use. Pour the batter onto a hot waffle iron and bake until brown using the manufacturer's directions.

Because of their high fat content, nuts spoil fast when exposed to heat, air, or light. Keep nuts, beans, and grains stored in airtight containers in a cool place, such as the refrigerator or basement. Shelled nuts keep for up to a month, unshelled, for four months (freeze them for longer storage). Dried beans will keep in a cool place for up to a year, and grains will keep indefinitely.

NUTRIENTS PER SERVING — Yield: 6 servings

CAL	PROT	CARBO	T FAT	SAT. FAT	MONOUFA	FIBER	SOD	OMEGA-3 FA	K
271	11G	18G	18G	2G	6G	5G	233MG	3G	298MG

PER SERVING	CARB CHOICES	1	CARB SOURCES					

sides
and
breads

Spices and herbs, fruits and vegetables,

pastas and grains—these sides will

complement any of the COOKING FOR LIFE

entrées. They are full of flavor and full of

healthy vitamins and minerals.

Vitamin C is thought to reduce the risk of eye cataracts, some cancers, and cardiovascular disease. Rich sources are green and red bell peppers (and other peppers or capsicums), broccoli, collard greens, spinach, tomatoes, potatoes, oranges and other citrus fruits, and strawberries.

Asparagus with Confetti Vinaigrette

1 1/2 **pounds fresh asparagus**

2 **large red bell peppers, finely chopped**

2 **large yellow bell peppers, finely chopped**

4 **scallions, thinly sliced**

2 **teaspoons chopped fresh thyme, or 1/2 teaspoon dried thyme**

1/3 **cup reduced-sodium chicken broth**

3 **tablespoons white wine vinegar**

1/2 **teaspoon pepper**

Snap off the thick woody ends of the asparagus spears. Bring 1/2 inch of water to a simmer in a large skillet over medium-high heat. Add the asparagus spears to the hot water and simmer for 3 to 4 minutes or until the asparagus is tender. Remove the asparagus to a serving platter with tongs. Drain the skillet.

Wipe the skillet dry with paper towels and spray with nonstick cooking spray. Sauté the bell peppers in the prepared skillet over medium-high heat for 4 minutes or until tender. Stir in the scallions and thyme and cook for 1 minute. Add the broth and vinegar and bring to a simmer. Season with the pepper and pour the hot vinaigrette over the asparagus.

NUTRIENTS PER SERVING   **Yield: 4 servings**

CAL	PROT	CARBO	T FAT	SAT. FAT	MONOUFA	FIBER	SOD	OMEGA-3 FA	K
91	6G	20G	1G	<1G	<1G	6G	56MG	<1G	781MG

PER SERVING	CARB CHOICES	1	CARB SOURCES				

Red Beans with Rice

1	pound dried red kidney beans	1/4	teaspoon cayenne pepper
6	cups water	1	green bell pepper, chopped
4	slices bacon, or 6 ounces salt pork	1/2	teaspoon coarse salt
1/2	cup chopped onion	1/4	teaspoon freshly ground black pepper
1	leek, cut into halves lengthwise and thinly sliced crosswise	2	cups basmati rice, cooked
2	ribs celery, thinly sliced crosswise		
1	teaspoon thyme		

Sort and rinse the beans. Combine the beans, water, bacon, onion, leek, celery, thyme and cayenne pepper in a 5-quart slow cooker. Cook, covered, on High for 4 hours or until the beans are tender; do not remove the cover during the cooking process. Stir in the bell pepper, salt and pepper.

Cook, covered, for 20 minutes longer or until the bell pepper is tender. Discard the bacon, if desired, and stir in the rice. Ladle into bowls.

Nutritional profile includes the bacon.

NUTRIENTS PER SERVING   Yield: 8 servings

CAL	PROT	CARBO	T FAT	SAT. FAT	MONOUFA	FIBER	SOD	OMEGA-3 FA	K
307	17G	55G	1G	‹1G	1G	15G	222MG	‹1G	104MG

PER SERVING	CARB CHOICES	3 1/2	CARB SOURCES				

Maple-Glazed Carrots

1	**pound baby carrots, julienned**	**1**	**teaspoon butter**
1	**tablespoon fresh lemon juice**	**1/8**	**teaspoon cinnamon**
1	**tablespoon light maple syrup**	**1/8**	**teaspoon pepper, or to taste**

Steam the carrots in a steamer for 4 to 6 minutes or until tender-crisp; drain. Cover to keep warm. Combine the lemon juice, maple syrup, butter, cinnamon and pepper in a saucepan.

Cook just until the butter melts, stirring occasionally. Add the carrots to the maple syrup mixture and toss to coat. Serve immediately.

NUTRIENTS PER SERVING   **Yield: 6 servings**

CAL	PROT	CARBO	T FAT	SAT. FAT	MONOUFA	FIBER	SOD	OMEGA-3 FA	K
41	1G	9G	1G	‹1G	‹1G	1G	59MG	‹1G	189MG

PER SERVING	CARB CHOICES	0	CARB SOURCES				

Eggplant Torta

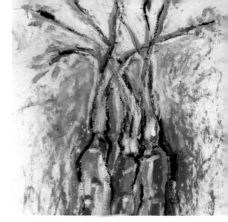

Seasoned Oil

1/3   **cup olive oil**

1   **garlic clove, chopped**

1   **teaspoon chopped fresh thyme, or
1/3 teaspoon dried thyme**

Torta

2   **(2-pound) eggplant, cut into
1/2 inch slices**

1/2   **teaspoon salt**

2   **(8-ounce) potatoes, peeled and
cut into 3/8-inch slices**

2   **tomatoes, cut into 3/8-inch slices**

1   **red onion, cut into 3/8-inch slices**

3/4   **cup torn fresh basil leaves**

     Sprigs of thyme (optional)

1/2   **teaspoon salt**

1/4   **teaspoon freshly ground pepper**

For the oil, whisk the olive oil, garlic and thyme in a bowl until combined.

For the torta, sprinkle the eggplant slices with 1/2 teaspoon salt and let stand for 1 hour. Rinse and pat dry with paper towels. Heat a large cast-iron skillet over high heat for 3 minutes. Brush the eggplant slices with some of the seasoned oil and sauté the slices in batches in the hot skillet for 2 to 3 minutes per side or until crusty and dark brown. Do not crowd the skillet and decrease the heat if the eggplant is browning too quickly.

Brush the sides and bottom of a baking pan with some of the remaining seasoned oil. Overlap the eggplant, potatoes, tomatoes and onion (leaving 1/2 inch of each uncovered) in the prepared baking pan, repeating the layers until all of the ingredients have been used, adding the basil and thyme between each layer.

Stir 1/2 teaspoon salt and the pepper into the remaining seasoned oil and brush over the top of the prepared layers. Bake at 350 degrees for 1 hour. Serve hot or at room temperature.

NUTRIENTS PER SERVING   **Yield: 8 servings**

CAL	PROT	CARBO	T FAT	SAT. FAT	MONOUFA	FIBER	SOD	OMEGA-3 FA	K
151	3G	17G	9G	1G	7G	6G	296MG	‹1G	623MG

PER SERVING	CARB CHOICES	1	CARB SOURCES				

Two-Potato Gratin

1	garlic clove, cut into halves		1/2	teaspoon salt
1	teaspoon olive oil		1/4	teaspoon freshly ground pepper
3	Yukon gold or red potatoes, peeled and cut into 1/8-inch slices (1 1/4 pounds)		1 1/4	cups skim milk
			1/8	teaspoon nutmeg
1	(8-ounce) sweet potato, peeled and cut into 1/8-inch slices		1	(1-ounce) slice whole wheat bread, torn
1	tablespoon butter, melted		2 1/2	teaspoons olive oil

Rub the cut sides of the garlic over the bottom and sides of a large gratin dish or shallow 1 1/2-quart baking dish. Lightly coat the bottom and sides of the dish with 1 teaspoon olive oil. Arrange 1/2 of the Yukon gold potato slices in a single layer in the bottom of the prepared dish and top with 1/2 of the sweet potato slices. Drizzle with the melted butter and sprinkle with 1/4 teaspoon of the salt and 1/8 teaspoon of the pepper. Top with the remaining Yukon gold potato slices, remaining sweet potato slices, remaining 1/4 teaspoon salt and remaining 1/8 teaspoon pepper.

Bring the skim milk and nutmeg to a boil in a saucepan. Remove from the heat and pour the hot milk mixture over the prepared layers. Process the bread in a food processor or blender until small crumbs form. Add 2 1/2 teaspoons olive oil to the crumbs and pulse to blend. Sprinkle the bread crumb mixture over the top and bake at 425 degrees for 45 to 50 minutes or until the potatoes are tender. Let stand for 5 minutes before serving.

NUTRIENTS PER SERVING   Yield: 6 servings

CAL	PROT	CARBO	T FAT	SAT. FAT	MONOUFA	FIBER	SOD	OMEGA-3 FA	K
171	5G	29G	5G	2G	3G	3G	254MG	<1G	701MG

PER SERVING	CARB CHOICES	2	CARB SOURCES				

Potato Chips

1 tablespoon plus 2 teaspoons unsalted butter	1/2 teaspoon fine sea salt
1 pound Idaho potatoes or sweet potatoes	

Melt the butter in a small saucepan over low heat. Heat until the butter stops foaming and becomes clear and clarified, with some solids floating on the top. Skim off the solids and discard.

Peel the potatoes and cut into 1/16-inch-thick rounds with a mandoline or vegetable slicer. Place the potatoes immediately into cold water in a bowl. Rinse the potatoes in several changes of cold water. Drain well and spin in a salad spinner. Do not leave the potatoes in the water for more than 5 minutes or they will curl up and won't cook evenly. (When using sweet potatoes, you must first blanch in 3 quarts of salted boiling water in a saucepan for 45 seconds so the sweet potatoes will brown evenly before continuing. Drain and cool under cold running water. Drain well or spin in a salad spinner.)

Pat the potatoes dry with paper towels and place in a medium bowl. Spoon the clear clarified butter onto the potatoes with a teaspoon, leaving the milky residue in the bottom of the saucepan. Toss the potatoes with the butter using a lightly dampened brush, making sure each slice is coated. Arrange the potato slices in a single layer on a large heavy baking sheet, making sure the edges do not touch each other.

Bake at 425 degrees on the middle oven rack for 7 minutes. Remove any potatoes that have become golden brown and crisp with a spatula to a platter lined with paper towels. Continue baking the remaining potato slices up to 3 minutes longer, checking frequently and removing any brown and crisp ones. Do not allow the potatoes to get very brown or they will become bitter. Sprinkle with the salt. Store in an airtight container for up to 2 days.

Fruits and vegetables provide fiber as well as vitamins and minerals, such as potassium, vitamin C, vitamin A (as carotenoids), folic acid, and a variety of disease-fighting phytonutrients.

NUTRIENTS PER SERVING   Yield: 4 servings

CAL	PROT	CARBO	T FAT	SAT. FAT	MONOUFA	FIBER	SOD	OMEGA-3 FA	K
144	2G	20G	6G	4G	0G	2G	295MG	<1G	616MG

PER SERVING	CARB CHOICES	1	CARB SOURCES				

Spinach and Mushrooms
with Feta Cheese

3   garlic cloves, sliced

2   tablespoons olive oil

1   cup sliced fresh mushrooms

3   tablespoons water or
    vegetable stock

2   pounds fresh spinach, stems
    removed (12 cups)

3   tablespoons feta cheese or
    sesame seeds (optional)

    Salt and freshly ground pepper
    to taste

Sauté the garlic in the olive oil in a large sauté pan over medium heat until softened. Add the mushrooms and cook for 1 minute, stirring once or twice. Add the water and spinach, rotating the spinach with tongs so that all the leaves are coated with the cooking juices.

Cook just until the spinach turns bright green and is thoroughly wilted. Sprinkle each serving with feta cheese and season with salt and pepper. Serve immediately.

NUTRIENTS PER SERVING   **Yield: 4 servings**

CAL	PROT	CARBO	T FAT	SAT. FAT	MONOUFA	FIBER	SOD	OMEGA-3 FA	K
120	7G	10G	8G	1G	5G	5G	180MG	<1G	1339MG

PER SERVING	CARB CHOICES	0	CARB SOURCES					

Better-for-You Macaroni and Cheese

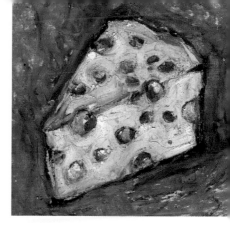

1	(1-pound) butternut squash, peeled and cut into 1-inch cubes (about 3 cups)
1¹/₂	cups skim milk
1	cup homemade or low-sodium chicken stock, skimmed
¹/₂	teaspoon coarse salt
¹/₈	teaspoon freshly grated nutmeg
¹/₈	teaspoon cayenne pepper
¹/₈	teaspoon freshly ground black pepper
16	ounces whole wheat elbow macaroni
4	ounces extra-sharp Cheddar cheese, finely shredded
¹/₂	cup part-skim ricotta cheese
¹/₄	cup (1 ounce) finely grated Parmesan cheese
2	tablespoons fine bread crumbs
1	teaspoon olive oil

Combine the squash, skim milk and stock in a medium saucepan and bring to a boil over medium-high heat. Reduce the heat to medium and simmer for 20 minutes or until the squash is tender when pierced with a fork. Remove from the heat and mash the squash mixture until smooth. Stir in the salt, nutmeg, cayenne pepper and black pepper.

Cook the pasta using the package directions for 8 minutes or until al dente; drain. Combine the pasta, squash mixture, Cheddar cheese, ricotta cheese and 2 tablespoons of the Parmesan cheese in a bowl and mix gently. Spoon the squash mixture into a 9x9-inch baking pan lightly sprayed with nonstick cooking spray.

Toss the bread crumbs, olive oil and remaining 2 tablespoons Parmesan cheese in a bowl and sprinkle evenly over the squash mixture. Bake, covered with foil, at 375 degrees for 20 minutes. Remove the foil and bake for 30 to 40 minutes longer or until light brown and crisp. Serve immediately.

Al dente: An Italian phrase meaning "to the tooth," describing pasta or other food that is cooked only until it offers a slight resistance when bitten.

NUTRIENTS PER SERVING | Yield: 6 servings

CAL	PROT	CARBO	T FAT	SAT. FAT	MONOUFA	FIBER	SOD	OMEGA-3 FA	K
455	22G	70G	11G	7G	2G	8G	426MG	<1G	559MG

PER SERVING	CARB CHOICES	4¹/₂	CARB SOURCES				

Spaghetti Squash

1	**(2-pound) spaghetti squash**	1/8	**teaspoon coarse salt**
1	**tablespoon butter, melted**	1/8	**teaspoon pepper**

Pierce the squash all over with a fork and arrange on a baking sheet. Bake at 400 degrees for 45 to 60 minutes or until the squash is easily pierced with the tip of a paring knife. Or microwave the pierced squash on High for 10 to 15 minutes.

Cut the squash into halves and discard the seeds. Using a fork gently scrape the flesh in a circular motion to release the strands and place in a bowl. Add the butter, salt and pepper and toss gently to mix. Serve immediately.

NUTRIENTS PER SERVING   Yield: 4 servings

CAL	PROT	CARBO	T FAT	SAT. FAT	MONOUFA	FIBER	SOD	OMEGA-3 FA	K
75	1G	11G	4G	2G	1G	0G	88MG	<1G	175MG

PER SERVING	CARB CHOICES	1	CARB SOURCES				

Parmesan Baked Tomatoes

4	plum tomatoes	1	tablespoon olive oil
1/4	cup (1 ounce) finely grated Parmesan cheese	1/2	teaspoon Italian herbs
2	tablespoons whole wheat bread crumbs	1/4	teaspoon salt
		1/8	teaspoon pepper

Slice the tomatoes lengthwise into halves and cut a sliver from the skin side of each half so the halves will lie flat. Arrange the tomato halves cut side up in a baking dish.

Toss the cheese, bread crumbs, olive oil, Italian herbs, salt and pepper in a bowl. Mound the bread crumb mixture evenly on the tomato halves and bake at 425 degrees for 20 minutes or until the tomatoes are tender and the topping is brown and crisp.

Food sources of antioxidants are favored over supplements. Food sources of vitamin C include citrus fruits, tomatoes, kiwifruit, peppers, and broccoli. Good sources of vitamin E include vegetable oils, wheat germ, avocados, almonds, peanuts, pistachios, and sunflower seeds.

NUTRIENTS PER SERVING   Yield: 4 servings

CAL	PROT	CARBO	T FAT	SAT. FAT	MONOUFA	FIBER	SOD	OMEGA-3 FA	K
66	3G	3G	5G	1G	3G	1G	233MG	<1G	157MG

PER SERVING	CARB CHOICES	0	CARB SOURCES	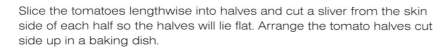

99

Garlic Bulgur with Herbs

2	tablespoons butter	2	garlic cloves, minced
1	cup chopped celery	1/4	teaspoon dill weed
1	onion, chopped	1/4	teaspoon oregano
1	cup fresh mushrooms, sliced	1/8	teaspoon basil
1	cup bulgur or cracked wheat		Coarse salt to taste
2	cups low-sodium chicken broth		

Melt the butter in a large skillet and stir in the celery, onion and mushrooms. Cook until the vegetables are tender, stirring constantly. Add the bulgur and cook until the bulgur is golden brown, stirring frequently. Stir in the broth, garlic, dill weed, oregano, basil and salt and cover. Bring to a boil and reduce the heat. Simmer for 15 minutes. Serve immediately.

NUTRIENTS PER SERVING   Yield: 8 servings

CAL	PROT	CARBO	T FAT	SAT. FAT	MONOUFA	FIBER	SOD	OMEGA-3 FA	K
106	4G	16G	4G	2G	1G	4G	34MG	<1G	218MG

PER SERVING	CARB CHOICES	1	CARB SOURCES				

Quinoa Stir-Fry

1/2	cup walnut pieces	6	ounces fresh baby spinach
1	cup quinoa	1	cup grape tomatoes or cherry tomatoes, cut into halves
2	tablespoons extra-virgin olive oil	1/3	cup freshly grated Parmigiano-Reggiano cheese
1	garlic clove, minced		Fresh basil leaves, torn
2	cups water		
1/2	teaspoon salt		

Spread the walnuts in a small skillet and toast over medium-low heat for 5 minutes or until light brown, stirring constantly. Remove the walnuts to a plate to cool. Combine the quinoa with enough water to cover in a bowl and swirl to rinse. Drain in a fine mesh strainer.

Heat the olive oil in a medium skillet and add the quinoa. Toast over medium heat for 10 minutes or until golden brown. Add the garlic and cook for 1 minute, stirring constantly. Stir in the water and salt and bring to a boil.

Reduce the heat to medium-low and cook, covered, for 15 minutes or until the water is absorbed. Stir in the spinach and tomatoes. Stir-fry over medium heat for 1 minute or until the spinach is almost wilted and the tomatoes are heated through. Stir in the walnuts and cheese. Spoon into a serving bowl and garnish with basil. Serve warm.

Look for the following first ingredient on the label to ensure you are getting whole grains: whole wheat, whole oats/oatmeal, whole grain corn, brown rice, whole rye, whole grain barley, wild rice, buckwheat, bulgur, millet, quinoa, and popcorn.

NUTRIENTS PER SERVING — Yield: 4 (1-cup) servings

CAL	PROT	CARBO	T FAT	SAT. FAT	MONOUFA	FIBER	SOD	OMEGA-3 FA	K
367	12G	35G	21G	3G	8G	5G	439MG	2G	712MG

PER SERVING	CARB CHOICES	2	CARB SOURCES				

When cooking something on the stovetop that might boil over, keep a large balloon whisk nearby to release the bubbles and lower the temperature of the overflowing liquid.

Sun-Dried Tomato Risotto

3	cups low-sodium chicken stock		1/4	teaspoon pepper
3	cups water		1/2	cup chopped drained oil-pack sun-dried tomatoes
3	tablespoons olive oil		1/4	cup chopped fresh basil
1	onion, chopped		1	tablespoon chopped fresh parsley
2	garlic cloves, minced		1/4	cup (1 ounce) freshly grated Parmesan cheese
1	cup risotto			
1 1/4	teaspoons salt			

Mix the stock and water in a bowl. Heat the olive oil in a saucepan over medium heat. Sauté the onion and garlic in the hot oil for 5 minutes or until the onion is tender. Stir in the risotto and sauté for 2 minutes or until the rice is crackling and begins to brown. Stir in 1 cup of the stock mixture, the salt and pepper and cook until the liquid is absorbed, stirring constantly. Add the sun-dried tomatoes, basil and parsley and mix well.

Add the remaining stock mixture 1 cup at a time and cook until the liquid is absorbed after each addition, stirring constantly. The risotto should be tender and slightly firm in the center with a creamy sauce. Stir in the cheese and serve immediately.

NUTRIENTS PER SERVING · Yield: 4 servings

CAL	PROT	CARBO	T FAT	SAT. FAT	MONOUFA	FIBER	SOD	OMEGA-3 FA	K
264	8G	27G	15G	3G	10G	1G	896MG	‹1G	440MG

PER SERVING	CARB CHOICES	2	CARB SOURCES				

Wild Rice Pilaf

2	tablespoons butter	4	cups low-sodium chicken broth
1/2	cup finely chopped onion	2	cups cooked wild rice
1 1/2	cups basmati rice	2	teaspoons fresh lemon juice

Melt the butter in a heavy 2-quart saucepan with a tight fitting lid over medium-low heat. Add the onion to the butter and sauté for 3 to 5 minutes or until tender. Add the basmati rice and stir until coated with the butter.

Bring the broth to a boil in a medium saucepan and stir the hot broth into the rice mixture. Cook, covered, over low heat for 15 minutes. Remove from the heat and let stand, covered, for 10 minutes. Fold in the wild rice and lemon juice. Serve immediately.

NUTRIENTS PER SERVING   Yield: 8 servings

CAL	PROT	CARBO	T FAT	SAT. FAT	MONOUFA	FIBER	SOD	OMEGA-3 FA	K
150	5G	25G	4G	2G	1G	1G	38MG	<1G	161MG

PER SERVING	CARB CHOICES	1 1/2	CARB SOURCES				

Lentils and Rice with Caramelized Onions

1½ teaspoons olive oil	1 cup lentils, sorted and rinsed
½ onion, chopped	3 cups low-sodium chicken stock
½ teaspoon minced garlic	½ cup basmati rice
½ teaspoon cumin	4½ teaspoons olive oil
⅛ teaspoon salt	1 onion, cut into halves and sliced
⅛ teaspoon pepper	Minced fresh parsley

Heat 1½ teaspoons olive oil in a large deep saucepan over medium heat for 1 minute. Add the chopped onion to the hot oil and cook for 5 minutes or just until it begins to soften. Stir in the garlic, cumin, salt and pepper and cook for 3 minutes longer, stirring occasionally. Add the lentils and mix well. Stir in 2 cups of the broth.

Cook for 20 minutes or until the lentils begin to soften, stirring occasionally. Add enough of the remaining stock to cover the lentils by 1 inch and stir in the rice. Reduce the heat to low and cook, covered, for 20 minutes longer or until the rice and lentils are tender and the liquid is absorbed. If the lentils and rice are not cooked through, add the remaining stock and cook, covered, for a few more minutes. If the lentils and rice are tender and there is liquid remaining, remove the cover, increase the heat and cook until the liquid is absorbed, stirring frequently. Remove from the heat and cover to keep warm.

Heat 4½ teaspoons olive oil in a medium skillet over medium-high heat. Add the sliced onion and cook for 15 minutes or until dark brown, stirring frequently. Remove the onion to a paper towel to drain. Spoon the caramelized onion over the rice and lentils in a bowl. Sprinkle with parsley.

NUTRIENTS PER SERVING   Yield: 4 servings

CAL	PROT	CARBO	T FAT	SAT. FAT	MONOUFA	FIBER	SOD	OMEGA-3 FA	K
297	16G	43G	8G	1G	5G	8G	143MG	<1G	574MG

PER SERVING	CARB CHOICES	3	CARB SOURCES				

Curried Vegetable Couscous

1	(4-inch) rib celery, cut into 1-inch pieces	1	tablespoon extra-virgin olive oil
1	(4-inch) carrot, peeled and cut into 1-inch pieces	1	teaspoon curry powder
1/2	yellow onion, coarsely chopped	1	cup (6 ounces) whole wheat couscous
1/2	red bell pepper, coarsely chopped	2	cups chicken or vegetable stock or broth
1	(1/4-inch) piece fresh ginger 1 inch in diameter, thinly sliced	1/2	teaspoon salt
1	garlic clove	2	tablespoons chopped fresh cilantro

Pulse the celery, carrot, onion, bell pepper, ginger and garlic in a food processor until the vegetables are finely minced; do not purée. Heat the olive oil in a large nonstick sauté pan or skillet over medium heat. Add the minced vegetable mixture to the hot oil and sauté for 3 minutes or until the vegetables begin to soften. Stir in the curry powder and sauté for 1 minute or until fragrant. Add the couscous and stock and mix well.

Bring the couscous mixture to a boil over high heat. Reduce the heat to low and cook, covered, for 5 minutes. Remove from the heat and fluff the couscous with a fork. Stir in the salt and cilantro and spoon into a serving bowl. Serve immediately.

Different vegetables are rich in different nutrients. For optimal nutrition, choose a variety of dark green vegetables, orange vegetables, legumes (dried beans), starchy vegetables, and other vegetables each week.

NUTRIENTS PER SERVING — Yield: 6 servings

CAL	PROT	CARBO	T FAT	SAT. FAT	MONOUFA	FIBER	SOD	OMEGA-3 FA	K
130	5G	20G	4G	1G	2G	3G	315MG	<1G	151MG

PER SERVING	CARB CHOICES	1	CARB SOURCES				

When it comes to pasta sauce, red is better. Marinara sauce generally has less fat than the white (Alfredo) sauce and contains lycopene, a carotenoid linked to a lower risk of heart disease and prostate cancer. Try adding extra chopped vegetables to purchased tomato sauce to increase the fiber and nutrition. Portion control is important with pasta—1 cup of cooked pasta contains 40 to 45 grams of carbohydrate.

Toasted Orzo with Olives and Lemons

3/4 teaspoon olive oil	1/8 teaspoon freshly ground pepper
8 ounces orzo (1 1/4 cups)	1/2 cup chopped black olives
2 cups water	2 tablespoons chopped fresh parsley
1 teaspoon grated lemon zest	1 tablespoon fresh lemon juice
1/8 teaspoon coarse salt	1 tablespoon olive oil

Heat 3/4 teaspoon olive oil in a large saucepan over medium-high heat. Add the pasta to the hot oil and sauté for 5 to 7 minutes or until golden brown. Stir in the water, lemon zest, salt and pepper and bring to a boil. Reduce the heat to medium.

Simmer, covered, for 10 to 15 minutes or until the pasta is al dente and the liquid is absorbed. If the pasta is tender but the liquid remains, cook uncovered until the liquid evaporates. Remove the pasta from the heat and stir in the olives, parsley, lemon juice and 1 tablespoon olive oil.

NUTRIENTS PER SERVING **Yield: 8 servings**

CAL	PROT	CARBO	T FAT	SAT. FAT	MONOUFA	FIBER	SOD	OMEGA-3 FA	K
134	4G	22G	3G	‹1G	2G	1G	106MG	‹1G	55MG

PER SERVING	CARB CHOICES	1 1/2	CARB SOURCES				

Cranberry Orange Bread

1	pound fresh cranberries	2	teaspoons baking powder
2	oranges, seeded	1/2	teaspoon salt
2	cups sugar	2	Omega-3-enhanced eggs, beaten
3	cups sifted all-purpose flour	2	tablespoons butter, melted
1	cup sifted whole wheat flour	2	teaspoons vanilla extract
2	teaspoons baking soda	1	cup walnuts, chopped

Combine the cranberries and oranges in a food processor and pulse until coarsely ground. Mix the cranberry mixture with the sugar in a bowl. Let stand at room temperature for 2 hours. Grease two 4×8-inch loaf pans and line with greased waxed paper. Sift the all-purpose flour, whole wheat flour, baking soda, baking powder and salt into a bowl and mix well.

Combine the cranberry mixture, eggs, butter and vanilla in a bowl and mix well. Stir in the walnuts. Add the cranberry mixture to the flour mixture and mix just until moistened. Spoon 1/2 of the cranberry mixture into each prepared loaf pan and bake, covered with foil, at 350 degrees for 20 minutes. Remove the foil and bake for 40 minutes longer. Immediately remove the loaves to a wire rack and discard the waxed paper. Let stand until cool.

NUTRIENTS PER SLICE — Yield: 2 dozen slices

CAL	PROT	CARBO	T FAT	SAT. FAT	MONOUFA	FIBER	SOD	OMEGA-3 FA	K
196	4G	36G	5G	1G	1G	3G	201MG	<1G	100MG

PER SERVING	CARB CHOICES	2	CARB SOURCES				

Nectarine Blueberry Bread

2/3 **cup chopped almonds**

1 **tablespoon sugar**

1 **cup unbleached all-purpose flour**

3/4 **cup sugar**

2 **teaspoons baking powder**

1/2 **teaspoon allspice**

1/4 **teaspoon baking soda**

1/4 **teaspoon salt**

1/3 **cup butter, softened**

1/4 **cup orange juice**

1 **teaspoon finely shredded orange zest**

1/2 **cup whole wheat flour**

2 **Omega-3-enhanced eggs**

1 **nectarine or peeled peach, coarsely chopped (about 2/3 cup)**

1 **cup fresh blueberries**

Combine 1/4 cup of the almonds and 1 tablespoon sugar in a bowl and mix well. Mix the all-purpose flour, 3/4 cup sugar, the baking powder, allspice, baking soda and salt in a mixing bowl. Add the butter, orange juice and orange zest and beat at low to medium speed for 30 seconds or until combined. Beat at high speed for 2 minutes, scraping the bowl occasionally. Add 1/2 cup whole wheat flour and the eggs and beat at low speed just until combined. Fold in the nectarine, blueberries and remaining almonds.

Spoon the batter into a greased 4x8-inch loaf pan and sprinkle with the almond mixture. Bake at 350 degrees for 55 to 60 minutes or until a wooden pick inserted near the center comes out clean. Cover with foil the last 15 minutes of the baking process to prevent overbrowning, if desired. Cool in the pan for 10 minutes. Remove to a wire rack to cool completely. Wrap the loaf in foil and let stand for 8 to 10 hours before slicing.

NUTRIENTS PER SLICE — Yield: 16 slices

CAL	PROT	CARBO	T FAT	SAT. FAT	MONOUFA	FIBER	SOD	OMEGA-3 FA	K
162	3G	22G	7G	3G	3G	2G	127MG	‹1G	98MG

PER SERVING	CARB CHOICES	1 1/2	CARB SOURCES					

Zucchini Parmesan Loaf

2	cups all-purpose flour
3/4	cup (3 ounces) grated Parmesan cheese
2	teaspoons baking powder
1 1/2	teaspoons coarse salt
1/4	teaspoon freshly ground pepper
8	ounces zucchini, coarsely grated (about 1 medium)
1/2	cup olive oil
1/3	cup milk
2	Omega-3-enhanced eggs

Combine the flour, cheese, baking powder, salt and pepper in a bowl and mix well. Stir in the zucchini. Whisk the olive oil, milk and eggs in a bowl until blended and add to the flour mixture, stirring just until moistened. The batter will be very thick, resembling biscuit dough.

Spoon the batter into a 5x9-inch loaf pan sprayed with nonstick cooking spray. Bake at 375 degrees for 60 to 70 minutes or until a wooden pick inserted in the center comes out clean; tent with foil to prevent overbrowning if necessary. Cool in the pan for 15 minutes. Remove to a wire rack to cool completely.

Omega-3s are related to lowering LDL (bad) cholesterol and triglycerides, increasing HDL (good) cholesterol, lowering blood pressure, decreasing inflammation, reducing blood clotting, and perhaps decreasing the risk of sudden cardiac death due to an irregular heartbeat. Omega-3s may also aid in diabetes control by making cells more sensitive to insulin.

NUTRIENTS PER SERVING
Yield: 6 servings

CAL	PROT	CARBO	T FAT	SAT. FAT	MONOUFA	FIBER	SOD	OMEGA-3 FA	K
392	11G	35G	23G	4G	15G	2G	829MG	<1G	198MG

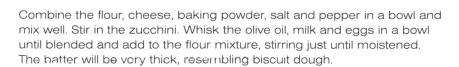

PER SERVING	CARB CHOICES	2	CARB SOURCES				

Brown Sugar Cornmeal Muffins

Brown Sugar Topping

1	tablespoon brown sugar
2	teaspoons white cornmeal

Muffins

2	cups all-purpose flour
1/2	cup packed brown sugar
1/4	cup white cornmeal

1	teaspoon baking powder
1	teaspoon baking soda
1	cup low-fat vanilla yogurt
1	Omega-3-enhanced egg
3	tablespoons skim milk
1	tablespoon trans-fat-free margarine, melted
1	teaspoon vanilla extract

For the topping, mix the brown sugar and cornmeal in a bowl.

For the muffins, combine the flour, brown sugar, cornmeal, baking powder and baking soda in a bowl and mix well. Add the yogurt, egg, skim milk, margarine and vanilla and mix just until moistened.

Divide the batter evenly among 12 muffin cups coated with nonstick cooking spray. Sprinkle evenly with the topping. Bake at 400 degrees for 17 minutes or until a wooden pick inserted in the centers comes out clean. Immediately remove the muffins to a wire rack to cool.

Use nonfat cooking sprays to coat baking dishes, baking pans, and muffin cups instead of greasing the pans with butter, oil, or solid shortening.

NUTRIENTS PER MUFFIN   Yield: 1 dozen muffins

CAL	PROT	CARBO	T FAT	SAT. FAT	MONOUFA	FIBER	SOD	OMEGA-3 FA	K
163	4G	32G	2G	<1G	<1G	1G	184MG	<1G	116MG

PER SERVING	CARB CHOICES	2	CARB SOURCES					

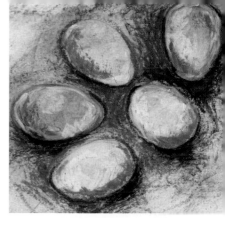

Herb Muffins

2   cups all-purpose flour

1   tablespoon baking powder

1/2 teaspoon salt

1/4 teaspoon freshly ground pepper

1   cup skim milk

1   Omega-3-enhanced egg

1/4 cup olive oil

1/2 cup (2 ounces) freshly grated
    Parmesan cheese

1/4 cup finely chopped
    sun-dried tomatoes

2   teaspoons chopped fresh thyme,
    oregano or dill weed, or
    1 teaspoon dried herb

Mix the flour, baking powder, salt and pepper in a bowl. Whisk the skim milk, egg and olive oil in a bowl until blended. Stir in the cheese, sun-dried tomatoes and thyme. Add the milk mixture to the flour mixture and stir just until moistened.

Fill 12 lightly buttered muffin cups 3/4 full. Bake at 375 degrees for 20 minutes or until a wooden pick inserted in the centers comes out clean. Cool in the pan for 3 minutes and remove the muffins to a wire rack.

NUTRIENTS PER MUFFIN   Yield: 1 dozen muffins

CAL	PROT	CARBO	T FAT	SAT. FAT	MONOUFA	FIBER	SOD	OMEGA-3 FA	K
149	5G	18G	6G	1G	4G	1G	286MG	<1G	64MG

| PER SERVING | CARB CHOICES | 1 | CARB SOURCES | | | | |

Pear, Ginger and Walnut Muffins

If a recipe calls for fresh ginger, shop for a piece with taut unwrinkled skin. Store ginger in the refrigerator.

1	cup unbleached all-purpose flour	2	Omega-3-enhanced eggs
1	cup whole wheat flour	2	tablespoons milk
3/4	cup sugar	1	teaspoon grated fresh ginger
2	teaspoons baking soda	2	pears, peeled and finely chopped
1	teaspoon cinnamon	3/4	cup chopped walnuts
1/2	teaspoon salt	1/2	cup raisins
1/2	cup canola oil		

Combine the all-purpose flour, whole wheat flour, sugar, baking soda, cinnamon and salt in a bowl and mix well. Make a well in the center of the flour mixture. Whisk the canola oil, eggs, milk and ginger in a bowl until combined. Add the oil mixture all at once to the well and stir just until moistened; the batter will be thick. Fold in the pears, walnuts and raisins.

Fill 18 lightly greased or paper-lined baking cups 3/4 full. Bake at 350 degrees for 20 to 25 minutes or until a wooden pick inserted in the centers comes out clean. Immediately remove to a wire rack. Serve warm.

NUTRIENTS PER MUFFIN — **Yield: 1 1/2 dozen muffins**

CAL	PROT	CARBO	T FAT	SAT. FAT	MONOUFA	FIBER	SOD	OMEGA-3 FA	K
197	3G	25G	10G	1G	4G	2G	128MG	1G	112MG

PER SERVING	CARB CHOICES	1 1/2	CARB SOURCES				

Fresh Raspberry Muffins

Walnut Topping

3   tablespoons chopped walnuts

2   tablespoons brown sugar

1   teaspoon cinnamon

Muffins

1¼ cups fresh raspberries

1   cup unbleached all-purpose flour

½   cup whole wheat flour

⅓   cup packed brown sugar

2   teaspoons baking powder

1   teaspoon cinnamon

¼   teaspoon salt

½   cup skim milk

¼   cup canola oil

1   Omega-3-enhanced egg, beaten

Confectioners' Sugar Glaze

¼   cup confectioners' sugar

2   teaspoons fresh lemon juice

For the topping, mix the walnuts, brown sugar and cinnamon in a bowl.

For the muffins, toss the raspberries and 2 tablespoons of the all-purpose flour in a bowl until coated. Combine the remaining all-purpose flour, whole wheat flour, brown sugar, baking powder, cinnamon and salt in a bowl and mix well. Whisk the skim milk, canola oil and egg in a bowl until blended. Stir the flour mixture into the egg mixture gradually. Fold in the raspberries.

Fill 12 muffin cups sprayed with nonstick cooking spray ⅔ full. Sprinkle with the topping and bake at 350 degrees for 20 to 25 minutes or until a wooden pick inserted in the centers comes out clean. Cool in the pan for 2 to 3 minutes and remove to a wire rack.

For the glaze, mix the confectioners' sugar and lemon juice in a bowl until of a glaze consistency. Drizzle over the slightly cooled muffins.

NUTRIENTS PER MUFFIN   **Yield: 1 dozen muffins**

CAL	PROT	CARBO	T FAT	SAT. FAT	MONOUFA	FIBER	SOD	OMEGA-3 FA	K
162	3G	24G	6G	‹1G	3G	2G	144MG	1G	100MG

PER SERVING	CARB CHOICES	1½	CARB SOURCES

Know the warning signs of hypoglycemia (low blood sugar) and how to treat it. If you feel shaky, sweaty, dizzy, or hungry, or if you have a headache or vision changes, check your blood sugar. Treat lows with the Rule of Fifteen—consume 15 grams of carbohydrate (1/2 cup juice or 1 cup milk), wait fifteen minutes, and then consume another 15 gram treatment if you do not feel better.

breads

Scones

1²/₃	cups all-purpose flour	¹/₃	cup sugar
2	teaspoons baking soda	¹/₂	cup (1 stick) butter, chilled and cut into pieces
2	teaspoons cream of tartar	1	cup buttermilk
¹/₈	teaspoon salt		
1²/₃	cups whole wheat flour		

Sift the all-purpose flour, baking soda, cream of tartar and salt into a large bowl and mix well. Stir in the whole wheat flour and sugar. Cut in the butter until crumbly. Stir in the buttermilk.

Knead the dough on a lightly floured surface for 30 seconds. Divide the dough into 2 equal portions and pat each portion into a 6-inch round. Cut each round into 4 wedges. Reassemble each of the wedges into 2 rounds on a baking sheet. Bake at 425 degrees for 12 minutes or until golden brown. Serve warm.

NUTRIENTS PER SCONE

Yield: 8 scones

CAL	PROT	CARBO	T FAT	SAT. FAT	MONOUFA	FIBER	SOD	OMEGA-3 FA	K
324	7G	48G	12G	7G	3G	4G	387MG	‹1G	303MG

PER SERVING	CARB CHOICES	3	CARB SOURCES				

Rosemary Focaccia

2	cups warm water		3	tablespoons water
2	envelopes dry yeast		3	tablespoons chopped fresh rosemary, or 1 teaspoon dried rosemary
1/4	cup extra-virgin ollve oil		1/2	teaspoon coarse salt
6	cups all-purpose flour			
1	tablespoon coarse salt			
1/4	cup extra-virgin olive oil			

Pour 2 cups warm water into a large mixing bowl and sprinkle with the yeast. Let stand for 5 minutes or until foamy. Stir in 1/4 cup olive oil. Mix the flour and 1 tablespoon salt in a bowl. Gradually add the flour mixture to the yeast mixture, beating constantly at low speed using a mixer fitted with a paddle attachment. Switch to the dough hook and knead at medium-high speed for 2 to 3 minutes or until the dough is smooth and slightly tacky. Place the dough in an oiled bowl and turn to coat. Let rise, covered with oiled plastic wrap, for 1 1/2 hours or until doubled in bulk.

Divide the dough into 2 equal portions and flatten each portion into a disk. Place each disk in the center of an oiled 9x12-inch baking sheet and pat each portion to fit the baking sheet. Cover with oiled plastic wrap.

Let rise for 1 hour. Make dimples in the top of each loaf by pinching with fingers. Mix 1/4 cup olive oil and 3 tablespoons water in a bowl and drizzle over the top of the loaves. Sprinkle with the rosemary and 1/2 teaspoon salt. Bake on the center oven rack at 450 degrees for 17 to 20 minutes or until golden brown. Cut each loaf into 2 dozen bite-size pieces.

NUTRIENTS PER PIECE — Yield: 4 dozen bite-size pieces

CAL	PROT	CARBO	T FAT	SAT. FAT	MONOUFA	FIBER	SOD	OMEGA-3 FA	K
79	2G	12G	3G	<1G	2G	1G	140MG	<1G	23MG

PER SERVING	CARB CHOICES	1	CARB SOURCES				

Tiramisu

1	cup cold water
1	(1-ounce) package sugar-free vanilla instant pudding mix
1/2	cup confectioners' sugar
8	ounces lite cream cheese, softened
1/4	cup fat-free half-and-half
8	ounces fat-free whipped topping
2	tablespoons coffee granules
3/4	cup hot water
24	ladyfingers, split lengthwise into halves
1	tablespoon baking cocoa

Whisk the cold water, pudding mix and confectioner's sugar in a mixing bowl until blended. Chill for 20 minutes. Beat the cream cheese and half-and-half in a mixing bowl until creamy. Add the cream cheese mixture to the pudding mixture and beat at medium speed until blended. Fold in the whipped topping.

Dissolve the coffee granules in the hot water in a heatproof bowl or mug. Layer the ladyfinger halves flat side down, coffee, pudding mixture and baking cocoa 1/3 at a time in a trifle bowl or large glass bowl. Chill, covered, for 4 hours or longer.

NUTRIENTS PER SERVING — Yield: 16 servings

CAL	PROT	CARBO	T FAT	SAT. FAT	MONOUFA	FIBER	SOD	OMEGA-3 FA	K
123	3G	21G	3G	1G	1G	<1G	110MG	0G	66MG

PER SERVING	CARB CHOICES	1	CARB SOURCES				

Lemon Custards with Fresh Blueberry Sauce

Lemon Custards

1	teaspoon canola oil
1¹/₂	cups plain soy milk
¹/₂	cup silken or soft tofu
3	Omega-3-enhanced eggs
2	tablespoons light brown sugar
2	tablespoons honey
2	teaspoons grated lemon zest
¹/₂	teaspoon lemon extract
¹/₂	teaspoon vanilla extract

Blueberry Sauce and Assembly

¹/₄	cup all-fruit blueberry preserves
2	tablespoons fresh lemon juice
³/₄	cup fresh blueberries

For the custards, lightly coat each of four ³/₄-cup custard cups with ¹/₄ teaspoon of the canola oil. Combine ¹/₂ cup of the soy milk and the tofu in a blender or food processor and process for 30 seconds or until smooth. Whisk the eggs in a bowl until blended. Stir in the brown sugar, honey, lemon zest and flavorings. Add the tofu mixture and remaining 1 cup soy milk to the egg mixture and whisk until blended.

Pour the custard mixture evenly into the prepared custard cups. Arrange the custard cups in a large baking pan. Pour enough hot water into the baking pan to come halfway up the sides of the custard cups. Bake at 300 degrees for 50 minutes or until set but the centers still jiggle slightly when gently shaken. Remove the custards from the water bath and let stand on a wire rack at room temperature for 15 minutes or until the custards are completely set. Chill, covered, for 4 hours or longer.

For the sauce, whisk the preserves and lemon juice in a bowl until combined. Fold in the blueberries. To serve, loosen the edges of the custards with the tip of a knife and invert the custards onto dessert plates. Drizzle each custard with ¹/₄ of the sauce. Or, simply top each custard with some of the sauce and place the custard cups on dessert plates.

Soy protein has been shown to reduce total cholesterol (4 to 5%) and LDL cholesterol (bad) (7%), to increase HDL cholesterol (good), to reduce formation of blood clots, and to protect kidney function. Soy milk should be fortified with calcium and vitamin D if used as a milk substitute. Check the Total Carbohydrate to determine how to fit it into a diabetes meal plan.

NUTRIENTS PER SERVING **Yield: 4 (³/₄-cup) servings**

CAL	PROT	CARBO	T FAT	SAT. FAT	MONOUFA	FIBER	SOD	OMEGA-3 FA	K
229	11G	32G	7G	‹1G	3G	3G	111MG	‹1G	281MG

PER SERVING	CARB CHOICES	2	CARB SOURCES					

Splenda starts out from table sugar but is processed so that the carbohydrate is not absorbed and changed into glucose. Up to four packets or eight teaspoons is considered a free food for people with diabetes. Splenda Granular measures cup for cup like sugar. Splenda Sugar Blend for Baking is twice as sweet as sugar, so only half as much is needed. Use 1/2 cup to replace a full cup of sugar in recipes.

Lemon Sorbet

4	cups plain yogurt	2	tablespoons chopped crystallized ginger
1/2	cup fresh lemon juice	1	teaspoon grated lemon zest
1/2	cup honey		

Combine the yogurt, lemon juice, honey, ginger and lemon zest in a blender and process until blended. Pour the sorbet mixture into a large bowl and freeze, covered, for 30 minutes or until thoroughly chilled. Pour the chilled sorbet mixture into an ice cream freezer container and freeze using the manufacturer's directions. Serve over fresh berries, such as blueberries, blackberries or raspberries, in dessert goblets.

Or, pour the sorbet mixture into a stainless steel bowl and freeze, covered, for 3 hours or until crystallized. Pulse in a food processor for 30 seconds. Return the sorbet mixture to the bowl and cover with plastic wrap. Freeze until solid.

NUTRIENTS PER SERVING									Yield: 12 servings
CAL	PROT	CARBO	T FAT	SAT. FAT	MONOUFA	FIBER	SOD	OMEGA-3 FA	K
97	3G	17G	2G	2G	1G	‹1G	36MG	‹1G	177MG

PER SERVING	CARB CHOICES	1	CARB SOURCES					

Berry **Parfait**

1 **cup fat-free blueberry yogurt**	1 **to 2 tablespoons fat-free granola**
1/2 **cup 1% cottage cheese**	1 **teaspoon crushed walnuts or almonds**
1/2 **cup fresh blueberries or sliced strawberries**	

Layer the yogurt, cottage cheese and blueberries in individual cups or dessert bowls. Sprinkle with the granola and walnuts.

NUTRIENTS PER SERVING   **Yield: 2 servings**

CAL	PROT	CARBO	T FAT	SAT. FAT	MONOUFA	FIBER	SOD	OMEGA-3 FA	K
154	12G	23G	2G	‹1G	‹1G	1G	298MG	‹1G	103MG

PER SERVING	CARB CHOICES **1 1/2**	CARB SOURCES

Baked Apples with Cherries and Almonds

1/3 cup (1 1/2 ounces) dried cherries, coarsely chopped	6 small Golden Delicious apples (1 3/4 pounds)
3 tablespoons chopped almonds	1/2 cup apple juice
1 tablespoon wheat germ	1/4 cup water
1 tablespoon brown sugar	2 tablespoons dark honey
1/2 teaspoon ground cinnamon	2 teaspoons walnut oil or canola oil
1/8 teaspoon nutmeg	

Toss the dried cherries, almonds, wheat germ, brown sugar, cinnamon and nutmeg in a bowl until combined. Peeling the apples is optional, but to peel in a decorative fashion, use a vegetable peeler or a sharp knife. Remove the peel from each apple in a circular motion, skipping every other row so that the rows of peel alternate with the rows of apple flesh. Working from the stem end, core each apple to within 3/4 inch of the bottom.

Press even amounts of the cherry mixture gently into the cavities and arrange the apples upright in a heavy ovenproof skillet or small baking dish just large enough to hold the apples.

Pour the apple juice and water into the skillet. Drizzle the honey and walnut oil over the apples and cover tightly with foil. Bake at 350 degrees for 1 hour or until the apples are easily pierced with a knife. Remove the apples to individual dessert plates and drizzle with the pan juices. Serve warm or at room temperature.

NUTRIENTS PER SERVING   Yield: 6 servings

CAL	PROT	CARBO	T FAT	SAT. FAT	MONOUFA	FIBER	SOD	OMEGA-3 FA	K
163	2G	32G	4G	‹1G	2G	4G	4MG	‹1G	192MG

PER SERVING	CARB CHOICES	2	CARB SOURCES				

Fresh Berry Applesauce

1	cup fresh raspberries	1	tablespoon lemon juice
1/2	cup fresh strawberries	5	whole cloves
1/4	cup water	1	(3-inch) cinnamon stick
1/4	cup packed brown sugar	5	cups coarsely shredded peeled Granny Smith apples
1/3	cup frozen apple juice concentrate, thawed		

Combine the raspberries, strawberries and water in a small saucepan and bring to a boil over medium-high heat. Boil for 2 minutes. Remove from the heat and mash. Strain the raspberry mixture through cheesecloth into a bowl, discarding the solids.

Combine the brown sugar, apple juice concentrate, lemon juice, cloves and cinnamon stick in a saucepan and bring to a boil over medium heat. Reduce the heat to low and simmer for 3 minutes, stirring occasionally. Stir in the apples and simmer, covered, for 30 minutes or until the apples are very tender, stirring occasionally. Remove from the heat and discard the cloves and cinnamon stick. Stir in the raspberry mixture and mash to the desired consistency. Serve warm or chilled in dessert bowls.

Eating whole fruits rather than drinking fruit juice is encouraged to help meet fiber recommendations. Whole fruit processes more slowly in the body than juices, providing satiety, and they are less likely to cause sharp increases in blood sugar.

NUTRIENTS PER SERVING　　　　　　　Yield: 9 (1/4-cup) servings

CAL	PROT	CARBO	T FAT	SAT. FAT	MONOUFA	FIBER	SOD	OMEGA-3 FA	K
71	‹1G	18G	‹1G	‹1G	‹1G	2G	3MG	‹1G	131MG

PER SERVING	CARB CHOICES	1	CARB SOURCES				

Apricot Berry Crumble

2 pounds firm ripe apricots, cut into halves	**³/₄** cup old-fashioned oats
8 whole almonds	**³/₄** cup packed light brown sugar
¹/₄ cup packed light brown sugar	**¹/₂** cup all-purpose flour
1¹/₂ teaspoons grated lemon zest	**¹/₂** cup whole wheat flour
1¹/₂ cups fresh raspberries	**1** tablespoon cinnamon
1¹/₂ cups fresh blueberries	**¹/₄** teaspoon salt
2 tablespoons fresh lemon juice	**¹/₂** cup (1 stick) plus 2 tablespoons butter, cut into tablespoons

Place the oven rack in the bottom third of the oven. Arrange the apricots in a shallow 2¹/₂-quart baking dish or 10-inch round baking dish. Process the almonds and ¹/₄ cup brown sugar in a food processor for 30 seconds. Add the lemon zest and process for 5 to 10 seconds. Scrape the brown sugar mixture over the apricots and toss to coat. Sprinkle the raspberries and blueberries over the apricot mixture and drizzle with the lemon juice.

Combine the oats, ³/₄ cup brown sugar, the all-purpose flour, whole wheat flour, cinnamon and salt in a food processor and process for 10 seconds. Add the butter and pulse just until crumbly. Sprinkle the crumb mixture evenly over the top and bake at 375 degrees for 55 minutes or until brown and bubbly. Remove to a wire rack to cool.

NUTRIENTS PER SERVING   Yield: 8 servings

CAL	PROT	CARBO	T FAT	SAT. FAT	MONOUFA	FIBER	SOD	OMEGA-3 FA	K
403	5G	64G	16G	9G	4G	7G	88MG	‹1G	533MG

PER SERVING	CARB CHOICES	**4**	CARB SOURCES	

Peach Brown Betty

2	(16-ounce) packages frozen sliced peaches, thawed	2	tablespoons all-purpose flour
1/2	cup sugar	4	slices whole wheat sandwich bread, torn
2	tablespoons fresh lemon juice	2	tablespoons butter

Toss the undrained peaches with the sugar, lemon juice and flour in a bowl until coated. Spoon the peach mixture into an 8x8-inch baking dish or shallow 2-quart baking dish. Process the bread in a blender until coarse crumbs form and sprinkle over the peach mixture. Dot with the butter.

Bake, covered tightly with foil, at 375 degrees for 25 to 30 minutes or until bubbly. Remove the foil and bake for 10 to 15 minutes longer or until golden brown. Let stand for 10 minutes before serving. Serve with whipped cream.

NUTRIENTS PER SERVING   Yield: 6 servings

CAL	PROT	CARBO	T FAT	SAT. FAT	MONOUFA	FIBER	SOD	OMEGA-3 FA	K
219	3G	40G	6G	3G	1G	5G	99MG	<1G	58MG

PER SERVING	CARB CHOICES	2 1/2	CARB SOURCES					

Potassium is a mineral that helps combat high blood pressure by maintaining the correct fluid balance in the body. Unless a doctor has restricted their potassium intake, most people do not get enough. Good sources are fruits and vegetables, such as bananas, apricots, oranges, prunes, sweet potatoes, baked potatoes with skin, tomatoes, milk, yogurt, dried beans, and fish.

desserts

Banana Galettes

2	(8-inch) whole wheat tortillas	3	tablespoons butter
1	teaspoon butter, melted	4	bananas, sliced diagonally into 1/4-inch slices
1/4	cup packed dark brown sugar		Vanilla frozen yogurt (optional)
1	tablespoon water		
1/2	teaspoon ground cinnamon		

Brush both sides of the tortillas with 1 teaspoon melted butter and arrange on a baking sheet. Bake at 450 degrees for 7 to 8 minutes or until golden brown, pressing with a spatula if the tortillas puff.

Combine the brown sugar, water and cinnamon in a saucepan and mix well. Add the butter and cook until the butter melts, stirring frequently. Arrange the sliced bananas in overlapping circles on the tortillas and brush evenly with the brown sugar mixture. Bake at 450 degrees for 10 minutes or until shiny. Cut each galette into 4 wedges and serve warm with frozen yogurt.

NUTRIENTS PER SERVING   Yield: 8 servings

CAL	PROT	CARBO	T FAT	SAT. FAT	MONOUFA	FIBER	SOD	OMEGA-3 FA	K
139	1G	25G	5G	3G	1G	2G	47MG	‹1G	257MG

PER SERVING	CARB CHOICES	1 1/2	CARB SOURCES				

Spiced Phyllo with Marinated Strawberries

3	cups fresh strawberries	4	sheets phyllo pastry
2	tablespoons honey	1/4	cup skim milk
2	teaspoons lemon juice	1/4	cup finely chopped almonds or walnuts
3/4	teaspoon cinnamon		
3	tablespoons confectioner's sugar		

Spray six 2³/₄-inch nonstick muffin cups or 6 individual nonstick molds with nonstick cooking spray. Cut the large strawberries into quarters. Combine the strawberries, honey, lemon juice and 1/2 of the cinnamon in a bowl and mix gently with a spatula. Mix the remaining cinnamon and confectioner's sugar in a bowl.

Lay 1 of the pastry sheets on a clean flat surface. Brush the sheet with some of the skim milk and sprinkle with 1/2 of the cinnamon and sugar mixture. Layer with another sheet of the pastry and sprinkle with the almonds. Stack with another sheet and brush with the remaining skim milk and sprinkle with the remaining cinnamon and sugar mixture. Top with the remaining pastry sheet. Cut the stack lengthwise into halves, then crosswise into 6 individual portions.

Cut 6 disks from the phyllo stack using a 6-inch round plate or upside-down custard cup as a guide. Mold each disk to fit into a muffin cup or mold. Bake at 350 degrees for 10 minutes or until brown and crisp. Cool in the pan. Spoon 1/2 cup of the strawberry mixture into each cup on a dessert plate. Serve at room temperature.

NUTRIENTS PER SERVING   Yield: 6 servings

CAL	PROT	CARBO	T FAT	SAT. FAT	MONOUFA	FIBER	SOD	OMEGA-3 FA	K
132	3G	23G	4G	‹1G	2G	2G	67MG	‹1G	181MG

PER SERVING	CARB CHOICES	1 1/2	CARB SOURCES				

To lower the fat in desserts, try substituting with one of the following: low-fat plain yogurt; low-fat sour cream; nonfat sour cream; buttermilk; evaporated skim milk; puréed fruits, such as bananas or pineapple, or cooked puréed fruits, such as dried dates, prunes, apricots, applesauce, and/or figs. A mixture of low-fat ricotta cheese or low-fat cottage cheese and a small amount of lite cream cheese is a good substitute for high-fat cream cheese.

Raspberry Almond Coffee Cake

Raspberry Filling

1	cup fresh raspberries
3	tablespoons brown sugar

Coffee Cake

1/2	cup unbleached all-purpose flour
1/2	cup whole wheat flour
1/3	cup sugar
1/2	teaspoon baking powder
1/4	teaspoon baking soda
1/8	teaspoon salt
1/2	cup low-fat plain yogurt

2	tablespoons butter, melted
1	Omega-3-enhanced egg, lightly beaten
1	teaspoon vanilla extract
1	tablespoon sliced almonds

Confectioners' Sugar Glaze

1/4	cup sifted confectioners' sugar
1	teaspoon skim milk
1/4	teaspoon vanilla extract

For the filling, toss the raspberries and brown sugar in a bowl.

For the coffee cake, combine the all-purpose flour, whole wheat flour, sugar, baking powder, baking soda and salt in a bowl and mix well. Mix the yogurt, butter, egg and vanilla in a bowl and add to the flour mixture, stirring just until moistened. Spread 2/3 of the batter in an 8-inch cake pan sprayed with nonstick cooking spray. Top with the filling and spread with the remaining batter. Sprinkle with the almonds. Bake at 350 degrees for 40 minutes or until a wooden pick inserted in the center comes out clean. Cool for 10 minutes.

For the glaze, mix the confectioners' sugar, skim milk and vanilla in a bowl until of a glaze consistency. Drizzle over the warm coffee cake. Serve warm or at room temperature.

NUTRIENTS PER SERVING

Yield: 8 servings

CAL	PROT	CARBO	T FAT	SAT. FAT	MONOUFA	FIBER	SOD	OMEGA-3 FA	K
171	4G	30G	4G	2G	1G	2G	129MG	‹1G	123MG

PER SERVING	CARB CHOICES	2	CARB SOURCES				

Orange Chiffon Cake

Cake

All-purpose flour for coating

1¹/₂ cups sifted cake flour

³/₄ cup granulated sugar

2 teaspoons baking powder

¹/₄ teaspoon salt

¹/₂ cup canola oil

¹/₂ cup fresh orange juice

1 teaspoon orange extract

3¹/₂ tablespoons orange zest

6 Omega-3-enhanced egg whites, at room temperature

2 tablespoons confectioners' sugar, sifted

Orange Glaze

1¹/₂ cups confectioners' sugar

1¹/₂ tablespoons orange juice

2 teaspoons lemon juice

For the cake, coat a 9-inch bundt pan with butter-flavor nonstick cooking spray and dust with all-purpose flour, tapping the pan lightly to remove excess flour. Sift the cake flour, granulated sugar, baking powder and salt into a large mixing bowl and mix well. Make a well in the center of the flour mixture and add the canola oil, orange juice, flavoring and 3 tablespoons of the orange zest to the well, reserving the remaining orange zest for the glaze. Do not mix. Beat the egg whites in a mixing bowl until foamy. Add the confectioners' sugar and beat until stiff but not dry peaks form. Do not rinse the beaters. Using the unrinsed beaters beat the flour mixture at medium-low speed until blended. Fold the batter in several batches into the egg whites. Spoon the batter into the prepared pan and smooth the top with a rubber spatula. Rap the pan sharply on the countertop to remove any large air bubbles. Bake at 350 degrees for 35 minutes or until golden brown and the top springs back when lightly touched. A wooden pick inserted in the center should come out clean. Cool in the pan on a wire rack for 10 minutes. Loosen the cake from the side of the pan using a long thin knife and invert onto a cake plate.

For the glaze, combine the confectioners' sugar, orange juice and lemon juice in a mixing bowl and beat until smooth. Adjust the consistency by adding more confectioners' sugar or juice if needed. The glaze should be thick but pourable. Drizzle over the top of the warm cake allowing the glaze to drip down the side. Sprinkle with the reserved orange zest.

NUTRIENTS PER SERVING   Yield: 16 servings

CAL	PROT	CARBO	T FAT	SAT. FAT	MONOUFA	FIBER	SOD	OMEGA-3 FA	K
210	3G	30G	9G	1G	5G	<1G	124MG	1G	57MG

PER SERVING	CARB CHOICES	2	CARB SOURCES				

Chocolate Carrot Cake

1	cup all-purpose flour
1	cup whole wheat flour
1/2	cup ground flaxseed
1/2	cup sugar
1/2	cup Splenda
1/2	cup baking cocoa
2	teaspoons baking soda
1	teaspoon ground cinnamon
1/2	teaspoon ground nutmeg
2	(6-ounce) cans juice-pack crushed pineapple
1/4	cup canola oil
1/4	cup puréed prunes or canola oil
3	Omega-3-enhanced eggs
2	cups shredded carrots

Combine the all-purpose flour, whole wheat flour, flaxseed, sugar, Splenda, baking cocoa, baking soda, cinnamon and nutmeg in a large mixing bowl and stir to mix well. Add the undrained pineapple, canola oil, puréed prunes, eggs and carrots and beat until blended. Pour into an oiled 10-inch tube pan. Bake at 350 degrees for 55 to 60 minutes or until the cake tests done. Cool in the pan for 10 minutes. Invert onto a serving plate to cool completely. Serve with lite whipped topping.

NUTRIENTS PER SERVING   Yield: 20 servings

CAL	PROT	CARBO	T FAT	SAT. FAT	MONOUFA	FIBER	SOD	OMEGA-3 FA	K
144	4G	23G	5G	1G	2G	3G	148MG	1G	131MG

PER SERVING	CARB CHOICES 1 1/2	CARB SOURCES				

desserts

Whether dessert comes at the end of the meal or as a special Saturday afternoon treat, it is a wonderful time to gather around the table with family and friends. Good conversation and good dessert— life doesn't get any sweeter!

Gingerbread with Rum Raisin Sauce

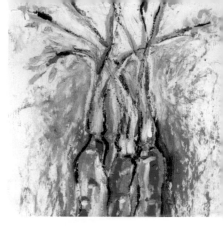

Gingerbread

1   cup all-purpose flour

1/4   cup whole wheat flour

1¹/₄ teaspoons ginger

3/4   teaspoon ground cinnamon

1/2   teaspoon ground cloves

1/2   teaspoon baking soda

1/4   teaspoon baking powder

1/4   teaspoon salt

1/3   cup packed brown sugar

1/4   cup (¹/₂ stick) reduced-calorie butter, softened

1/4   cup molasses

1   Omega-3-enhanced egg

1/2   cup buttermilk

Rum Raisin Sauce

3/4   cup skim milk

1   tablespoon sugar

1/2   teaspoon cornstarch

1   Omega-3-enhanced egg yolk, lightly beaten

1/4   cup raisins

1/2   teaspoon vanilla extract

1/2   teaspoon rum flavoring

To allow for a dessert at a meal, you may choose to "trade" other carbohydrate choices for the treats to stay within your goals.

For the gingerbread, combine the all-purpose flour, whole wheat flour, ginger, cinnamon, cloves, baking soda, baking powder and salt in a bowl and mix well. Beat the brown sugar, butter, molasses and egg in a large mixing bowl at medium speed until blended. Add the dry ingredients and buttermilk alternately to the egg mixture, beginning and ending with the dry ingredients and beating well after each addition. Spoon the batter into an 8x8-inch cake pan sprayed with nonstick cooking spray. Bake at 350 degrees for 35 minutes. Cool in the pan on a wire rack for 10 minutes.

For the sauce, whisk the skim milk, sugar and cornstarch in a small saucepan until blended. Cook over medium heat for 10 minutes or until thickened, stirring frequently. Stir 1/4 cup of the hot milk mixture into the egg yolk. Stir the egg yolk mixture into the hot milk mixture. Cook for 1 minute longer, stirring frequently. Add the raisins and flavorings and mix well. Serve warm with the gingerbread.

NUTRIENTS PER SERVING
Yield: 10 servings

CAL	PROT	CARBO	T FAT	SAT. FAT	MONOUFA	FIBER	SOD	OMEGA-3 FA	K
174	4G	31G	4G	2G	1G	1G	170MG	‹1G	258MG

PER SERVING	CARB CHOICES	2	CARB SOURCES				

Walnut Cappuccino Biscotti

1²/₃ cups all-purpose flour	¹/₄ cup strong coffee, cooled
²/₃ cup whole wheat flour	1 tablespoon 1% milk
1 cup sugar	1 Omega-3-enhanced egg
¹/₂ teaspoon baking soda	1 Omega-3-enhanced egg white
¹/₂ teaspoon baking powder	1 teaspoon vanilla extract
¹/₂ teaspoon ground cinnamon (optional)	³/₄ cup coarsely chopped toasted walnuts
¹/₂ teaspoon salt	¹/₂ cup chocolate chips

Mix the all-purpose flour, whole wheat flour, sugar, baking soda, baking powder, cinnamon and salt in a bowl. Whisk the coffee, 1% milk, egg, egg white and vanilla in a bowl until blended. Add the coffee mixture to the flour mixture and stir by hand just until a soft dough forms. Stir in the walnuts and chocolate chips.

Divide the dough into 2 equal portions and shape into two 8-inch logs on a lightly floured surface. Arrange the logs 2 to 3 inches apart on a cookie sheet coated with nonstick cooking spray. Flatten each log into a rectangle about 3 inches wide.

Bake at 350 degrees for 20 to 25 minutes or until golden brown and firm. Cool the logs on a wire rack for 15 minutes. Reduce the oven temperature to 275 degrees. Place the logs on a cutting board and trim the ends. Cut each log diagonally into ¹/₂- to ³/₄-inch slices using a serrated knife. Arrange the slices cut side down on the cookie sheet and bake for 20 minutes longer. Cool on the cookie sheet for 2 minutes. Remove to a wire rack to cool completely. Store in an airtight container.

NUTRIENTS PER BISCOTTI   Yield: 2 dozen biscotti

CAL	PROT	CARBO	T FAT	SAT. FAT	MONOUFA	FIBER	SOD	OMEGA-3 FA	K
120	3G	20G	4G	1G	1G	1G	91MG	‹1G	60MG

PER SERVING	CARB CHOICES	1	CARB SOURCES	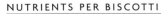

Orange Butter Cookies

Cookies

2/3 **cup butter, softened**

3/4 **cup sugar**

1 **Omega-3-enhanced egg**

**Grated zest of 1 large orange
(about 2 tablespoons)**

1/2 **cup orange juice**

2 **cups all-purpose flour**

1/2 **teaspoon baking powder**

1/2 **teaspoon baking soda**

1/2 **teaspoon salt**

Orange Butter Frosting

1 1/2 **cups confectioners' sugar**

2 **tablespoons butter, softened**

**Grated zest of 1 large orange
(about 2 tablespoons)**

1 1/2 **tablespoons orange juice**

For the cookies, combine the butter, sugar and egg in a large bowl and mix with a spoon until creamy and well blended. Stir in the orange zest and orange juice. Add the flour, baking powder, baking soda and salt and stir to mix well. Drop the dough by tablespoonfuls about 2 inches apart onto an ungreased cookie sheet. Bake at 350 degrees for 8 to 10 minutes or until light brown around the edges. Cool on the cookie sheet for 1 to 2 minutes. Remove to a wire rack and let stand for 30 minutes to cool completely.

For the frosting, combine the confectioners' sugar, butter, orange zest and orange juice in a bowl and mix until of a spreading consistency. Spread over the cooled cookies.

NUTRIENTS PER COOKIE · Yield: 3 1/2 dozen cookies

CAL	PROT	CARBO	T FAT	SAT. FAT	MONOUFA	FIBER	SOD	OMEGA-3 FA	K
86	1G	13G	4G	2G	1G	‹1G	51MG	‹1G	17MG

PER SERVING	CARB CHOICES	1	CARB SOURCES				

This Austrian cookie is typically made with almonds and raspberry jam, but a different nut or jam will work, too.

desserts

Classic Linzer Cookies

1²/₃	cups all-purpose flour	1	tablespoon grated lemon zest (optional)
1	teaspoon baking powder	1	Omega-3-enhanced egg
¹/₄	teaspoon salt	1	teaspoon vanilla extract
³/₄	cup granulated sugar	¹/₄	cup sliced almonds
¹/₄	cup (¹/₂ stick) trans-fat-free margarine or butter, softened	¹/₃	cup raspberry jam
1	tablespoon canola oil		Confectioners' sugar to taste

Mix the flour, baking powder and salt in a bowl. Beat the sugar, margarine, canola oil and lemon zest in a mixing bowl until light and fluffy. Add the egg and vanilla and beat until blended. Add the flour mixture and stir by hand just until a soft dough forms.

Divide the dough into 2 equal portions and shape each portion into a disk. Wrap each disk in plastic wrap and chill for 1 hour or until well chilled. Place 1 disk between 2 sheets of waxed paper dusted with flour. Roll ¹/₄ inch thick and cut with a 1¹/₂- to 2-inch round cutter or glass rim. Using a ¹/₂-inch round or shaped cutter cut the centers out of ¹/₂ of the rounds. Arrange the cookies 2 to 3 inches apart on a cookie sheet sprayed with nonstick cooking spray. Sprinkle the cookies with cut-out centers with almonds, pressing gently to ensure adherence. Bake at 350 degrees for 10 to 12 minutes or until the edges are light brown.

Cool on the cookie sheet for 2 minutes. Remove to a wire rack to cool completely. Repeat the process with the remaining dough disk, rerolling the scraps just once for more cookies. Spread the solid cookies with the jam and sprinkle the cut-out cookies lightly with confectioners' sugar. Top each solid cookie with a cut-out cookie. Store in an airtight container.

NUTRIENTS PER COOKIE								Yield: 2¹/₂ dozen cookies	
CAL	PROT	CARBO	T FAT	SAT. FAT	MONOUFA	FIBER	SOD	OMEGA-3 FA	K
79	1G	13G	3G	‹1G	1G	‹1G	59MG	‹1G	17MG

PER SERVING	CARB CHOICES	1	CARB SOURCES				

Carrot Pumpkin Bars

3/4	cup all-purpose flour
1/4	cup whole wheat flour
1	teaspoon baking powder
1/2	teaspoon ground cinnamon
1/4	teaspoon baking soda
1/4	teaspoon salt
1	Omega-3-enhanced egg
1	Omega-3-enhanced egg white
3/4	cup packed brown sugar
1/2	cup canned pumpkin

2	tablespoons trans-fat-free margarine or butter, melted
2	tablespoons canola oil
	Grated zest of 1 orange
1	teaspoon vanilla extract
1/2	cup packed grated carrots
1/3	cup raisins
1/3	cup dried cranberries or chopped dried apricots
1/3	cup chopped walnuts or pecans

Mix the all-purpose flour, whole wheat flour, baking powder, cinnamon, baking soda and salt in a bowl. Beat the egg and egg white in a mixing bowl until foamy. Add the brown sugar, pumpkin, margarine, canola oil, orange zest and vanilla and beat until smooth. Add the flour mixture and stir by hand just until moistened. Stir in the carrots, raisins, cranberries and walnuts.

Spread the batter in an 8x8-inch baking pan coated with nonstick cooking spray. Bake at 350 degrees for 30 to 35 minutes or until the top springs back when lightly touched. Cool in the pan on a wire rack and cut into bars. Store in an airtight container.

NUTRIENTS PER BAR   **Yield: 1 dozen bars**

CAL	PROT	CARBO	T FAT	SAT. FAT	MONOUFA	FIBER	SOD	OMEGA-3 FA	K
184	3G	29G	7G	1G	2G	2G	162MG	1G	142MG

PER SERVING	CARB CHOICES	2	CARB SOURCES				

Diets high in calcium cause fat cells to make less fat and help the body break down fat stores. Fat loss tends to come from the abdominal region. Making low-fat dairy a part of a healthy diet for weight control can enhance the benefits.

Sweet Potato Pie

1¹/₂ **pounds sweet potatoes**	1 **teaspoon vanilla extract**
1 **cup sugar**	¹/₂ **teaspoon nutmeg**
³/₄ **cup (1¹/₂ sticks) butter**	1 **unbaked (9-inch) pie shell**
2 **Omega-3-enhanced eggs**	

Combine the sweet potatoes with enough water to cover in a saucepan and bring to a boil. Boil for 20 to 30 minutes or until tender. Drain and peel the sweet potatoes.

Process the sweet potatoes, sugar and butter in a blender just until combined. Add the eggs, vanilla and nutmeg and process until smooth.

Spoon the sweet potato filling into the pie shell and bake at 375 degrees for 45 to 55 minutes or until set. Remove to a wire rack to cool.

NUTRIENTS PER SERVING **Yield: 8 servings**

CAL	PROT	CARBO	T FAT	SAT. FAT	MONOUFA	FIBER	SOD	OMEGA-3 FA	K
464	4G	57G	26G	13G	8G	3G	166MG	‹1G	266MG

PER SERVING	CARB CHOICES	4	CARB SOURCES				

Lemon Cream Tart

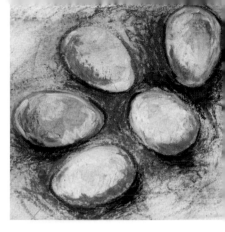

6	dozen vanilla wafers		2	Omega-3-enhanced eggs
6	tablespoons butter, melted		1/3	cup sugar
2	cups part-skim ricotta cheese		3	tablespoons fresh lemon juice (about 1 lemon)
4	ounces lite cream cheese, softened		2	tablespoons grated lemon zest (about 2 lemons)

Pulse the vanilla wafers in a food processor until finely ground. The crumbs should measure 2 cups. Toss the wafer crumbs and butter in a bowl. Press the crumb mixture over the bottom and up the side of a 9-inch tart pan with a removable bottom. Place the pan on a baking sheet and bake at 375 degrees for 10 to 12 minutes or until light brown. Maintain the oven temperature.

Combine the ricotta cheese, cream cheese, eggs, sugar, lemon juice and lemon zest in a food processor and process until blended. Spread the ricotta cheese mixture in the prepared tart pan and bake for 30 to 35 minutes or until the filling is set and browned in spots. Remove to a wire rack to cool completely.

NUTRIENTS PER SERVING   **Yield: 8 servings**

CAL	PROT	CARBO	T FAT	SAT. FAT	MONOUFA	FIBER	SOD	OMEGA-3 FA	K
467	14G	53G	23G	11G	4G	<1G	383MG	<1G	128MG

PER SERVING	CARB CHOICES	3 1/2	CARB SOURCES				

Index

YOUR ORDER	QTY	TOTAL
Cooking for Life, Volume 3 at $19.95 per cookbook		$
Shipping and handling $5.00 for 1 book and $1.00 for each additional book shipped to the same address		$
	Subtotal	$
South Dakota residents add 6% sales tax to subtotal (no tax if mailing outside of South Dakota)	Tax	$
	Total	$

Bill to:

Name _____

Street Address _____

City _____ State _____ Zip _____

Telephone ( ) _____ E-mail _____

Ship to: [ ] Same as billing address. (Please print. If multiple ship-to addresses, please attach to this form.)

Name _____

Street Address _____

City _____ State _____ Zip _____

Telephone ( ) _____ E-mail _____

Method of Payment: [ ] Check made payable to Avera McKennan Foundation
[ ] VISA [ ] MasterCard [ ] Discover
[ ] American Express

Name _____
(Print name as it appears on your charge card.)

Account # _____ Expiration Date (Mo/Yr) _____

Cardholder's Signature _____

Cookbook sale proceeds will be used to provide education and
services to individuals with diabetes.

Photocopies will be accepted.

COOKING
FOR *Life*

Avera McKennan
Foundation
800 East 21st Street
PO Box 5045
Sioux Falls, SD
57117-5045

Place your order today!

Call: 605-322-8900

Mail this form to: Avera
McKennan Foundation

Go online at www.avera
mckennanfoundation.org
to order COOKING FOR
LIFE cookbooks and
other customized gift
items that are perfect
for your own kitchen or
the kitchen of a friend
or loved one!

Avera
McKennan
Foundation